WALI

"HE SPELLED MY NAME CORRECTLY. THERE IS THAT."
– *Mrs. P. Traynor*

"BREATHTAKING PLOT-TWISTS, CHOCOLATE TRUFFLES
AND HONEST-TO-G*D POT-BELLIED PIGS"
– *Impressive National Newspaper*

"WHO DOES NURMI HUSA THINK HE IS?!
FOR THAT MATTER, WHO IS NURMI HUSA?!"
– *Famous Celebrity Interviewer*

"I'M SO MAD I COULD SPIT."
– *Not Quite So Famous Swedish Snoose Fancier*

"I'M THINKING OF SUING."
– *Well-known Radio Personality*

"YES, IT'S FUNNY - BUT ONLY IF YOU ACTUALLY *care*
FOR THAT SORT OF THING..."
– *Snobby Literary Reviewer*

"DEAD SQUIRRELS? WHAT'S SO DAMN
FUNNY ABOUT DEAD SQUIRRELS?"
– *Famous Actress & Animal Rights Campaigner*

"THE MAN IS CERTIFIABLE."
– *Mr. Husa's Former Therapist*

"PARTIAL SENTENCES! LOTS OF N-DASHES!"
– *International Journal of Spelling, Grammar & Punctuation*

"I HATED IT."
– *Famous Political Consultant*

waldo

a moral tale WITHOUT a moral

NURMI HUSA

vote4waldo.co.nr

Without the obstinate and unrelenting encouragement
(let alone financial and emotional support)
provided by friends and family
this book would never have been birthed.

So blame them, not me.

Elaine.
Blame her especially.

one

Once upon a time there was a middle-aged sweet shop owner named Waldo. He was an ordinary fellow, not remarkable in the least, except that he had a pleasant personality and was – on account of that, apparently – well-thought-of. Well, he was well-thought-of when anyone actually bothered to take the time to think of him. Which didn't happen all that often. Frankly, Waldo was the sort of fellow who was overlooked even when he was the only other person in the room. Truth be told, even Waldo was in the habit of overlooking himself. The man was one of those rare individuals who actually put the needs and thoughts of others before his own. And so when it came to pass that he and the various and sundry details of his here-to-fore exceedingly dull life exploded into an extravagant celebrity it proved such a shock for all concerned, with none more deeply horrified than the hapless Waldo himself.

It all began with an order for double mocha mint raspberry truffles with hazelnuts. Late one afternoon while filling the dentist's wife's weekly half-pound order, Waldo chanced to remark to her in the course of an otherwise unremarkable conversation, "You know, Mrs. Kepple, it's all a question of good neighborliness. When it comes to politics, why do we seem to forget that? It's cooperation, not conflict, that makes a community."

The artless simplicity with which this gem of uncommon common sense fell from his lips took the dentist's wife utterly by surprise. She peered at him with newfound interest. "That is an amazingly shrewd observation, Mr. Waldo," she noted keenly. "I wish we had more people like you on our village council. Perhaps things wouldn't be as nasty as they are."

Now it was Waldo's turn to be surprised. No one had ever suggested such a thing before – nor had it even occurred to him. To serve on the village council? "Nonsense!" he said to himself after she had left, and quite dismissed the silly notion from his thoughts.

•

But Mrs. Kepple didn't dismiss it from her thoughts. Far from it. The longer the idea bounced about in her brain, the better it seemed. The village needed someone like Waldo on the council – desperately. In a careful, off-hand manner, she deftly slid the idea in front of her husband at an early lunch the next day.

"Waldo?!" His eyebrows went up as his newspaper came down.

"That's right, dear, Waldo. You know Waldo. More tea?" She poured it even as she was asking. Dr. Kepple stared at his wife in astonishment.

"Waldo on the village council? Waldo?! I've never thought of Waldo in that way before."

"Well, neither had I until he said 'You know, Mrs. Kepple, it's all a question of good neighborliness. When it comes to politics, why do we seem to forget that? It's cooperation, not conflict, that makes a community.' It quite took my breath away."

"Waldo said that?"

"He did indeed."

"Waldo?!"

"Waldo."

"What utter nonsense."

"Yes, dear. . . "

"You do realize it's a hopelessly altruistic view of the world."

"Yes, but why must we always vote for quote hardheaded pragmatists unquote and mealy-mouthed panderers? Answer me that! Just for once I'd like to vote for a nice man, a *gentle* man, a man whose heart was in the right place. Someone I could trust implicitly to do the decent thing. Unlike that dreadful Councilor Millstone!"

"I see your point, my sweet. I've never much liked Millstone myself. He never says a wrong thing and never does a right one." Absent-mindedly he plopped two sugar cubes into his tea. "Waldo might just be the refreshing change we need."

"I trust your judgment, dear..." She moved the sugar bowl away from him before he could drop in a third. "So you'll have a word with Mr. Stieffel?" Mr. Stieffel, the local mortician, was widely regarded throughout the community as the soundest of sounding boards. If Stieffel pronounced upon a subject, it was definitively pronounced upon.

"Stieffel. Why, yes, of course, dear. Waldo on the village council? Oh my..." Chuckling quietly he finished his lunch and went over to the mortuary to have a word with Stieffel.

●

Stieffel was also greatly surprised, of course, by the outrageous idea.

"Waldo?! The sweet shop owner? Where in heaven's name did you get the idea of putting Waldo up for village council?" He laughed out loud.

"My wife, actually," muttered the dentist, left eyebrow raised. The mortician's laughter slickly transformed itself into a demure cough. He found some papers on his desk that desperately needed shuffling.

"Ah, yes, dear Mrs. Kepple!" Stieffel knew the dentist's wife and gave her a wide berth. As the President of the Ladies' Progressive Thought Society, she was a formidable moral force in the community. He viewed her many accomplishments with envy and not a little fear. "So what has so excited your lovely wife about old Waldo as a candidate?"

"A conversation they had the other day. He said to her 'You know, Mrs. Kepple, it's all a question of good neighborliness. When it comes to politics, why do we seem to forget that? It's cooperation, not conflict, that makes a community.' It quite took her breath away."

"Well, it's a hopelessly altruistic view of the world."

"Exactly what I said, Stieffel. Then she said to me, 'Why must we always vote for quote hardheaded pragmatists unquote and mealy-mouthed panderers? Just for once I'd like to vote for a nice man, a *gentle* man, a man whose heart was in the right place. Someone I could trust implicitly to do the decent thing.'"

Mr. Stieffel frowned thoughtfully. "I wouldn't argue with your lovely wife on that point. I've often felt that way myself."

"Me, too! Honestly, I think she may have something here."

"Hamm," mused the mortician, tapping his desk with a pencil. "A candidate who's just an ordinary fellow with a good heart? It's a dangerous concept. Radical. And yet, perhaps the time has come, my good Doctor, perhaps the time has come..." Stieffel gripped the pencil and waved it absent-mindedly.

"Yes," continued the dentist. "And just think who he'd could run against? That bastard Millstone."

"Millstone!" The mortician's pencil found itself suddenly snapped in half. The sharp crack startled Stieffel as well as Dr. Kepple.

"We should never have allowed him into our little development project," muttered the mortician peevishly as he tossed the now ruined pencil away.

The good doctor stared at the wastebasket glumly. "What choice had we?"

Stieffel swiveled his angry gaze out the window. A clump of overgrown rhododendrons glared back at him. They needed pruning. Badly. Why had he not noticed before? "Those measly tax write-offs he arranged weren't worth it. He ought to be turned out to pasture, the greedy old SOB."

"I couldn't agree with you more," insisted Dr. Kepple with admirable fellow-feeling.

Stieffel turned back and studied his good friend and business partner. A brilliant shaft of wintry sunlight sliced through the overcast sky and bounced abruptly across the mortician's desk. Was it that which produced such a disturbing glint in his eye? "Waldo, eh?" he murmured.

The dentist nodded gravely. "Waldo, indeed."

•

Waldo for Village Council – what a patently ridiculous idea! Even so, Mr. Stieffel deigned to speak to his friend Mr. Windsor, the banker. After mentioning it in staff meeting, Mr. Windsor had a quiet word with Bill, the barber, as he was having his weekly trim. But Bill had already heard about it from Mr. Randall of the unevenly receding hairline who had been apprised of the situation by the inevitably well-informed Mrs.

Randall who had run into Mrs. Van Penner at the grocer's who had spoken with Mr. Flick, the butcher, who had overheard his wife on the phone with old Mrs. Pedersen, the high school music teacher, who had by chance actually read the note the Guthrie girl was caught passing to the De Mornay boy. By three in the afternoon, Mr. Hering was on the phone to Waldo.

Mr. Hering was the editor, publisher, reporter, photographer and typesetter for the village's weekly newspaper *The Herald Sentinel Gazette*. Unfortunately, the answering machine at Waldo's sweet shop picked up, obliging Mr. Hering to leave a terse and vaguely threatening demand to "return his call immediately." Mr. Hering hated voice mail and answering machines. He felt had only been designed to give people an excuse to avoid talking to him in person. He took a deep breath, calmed down and tried Mrs. Waldo at home. Happily, she answered the phone. Did she have any comment regarding her husband's candidacy?

"Candy Daisies? My husband is selling Candy Daisies? How charming. I love daisies." Mrs. Waldo had been cleaning the tub and the cleaning fluid fumes had made her a little dizzy.

"No, no, Mrs. Waldo, candidacy, not Candy Daisies. Your husband is running for village council on the reform ticket, is he not?" Mrs. Waldo laughed out loud at the ridiculous idea. "So, you find his candidacy laughable? Interesting…" Mr. Hering made a note and underlined it. "Why is that? Don't you support his candidacy?"

"My husband is a candidate for village council? This is the first I've heard of it."

"So, he told you nothing about it? Interesting…" Mr. Hering made another note and circled it.

"You must have him mixed up with Mr. Waldorf, the dry cleaner. Mr. Waldorf is very interested in politics. The last time I went in with some cleaning he bent my ear for nearly three-quarters of an hour regarding some sort of sinister link between the rise in local sewer assessments and some mission that dries laterally – which made absolutely no sense –."

"You mean the Tri-Lateral Commission? Interesting…" This interview was opening up very successfully, thought Mr. Hering, as he made yet another note and underlined it twice.

"Well, he may have meant it, but as I said, it made no sense to me. Anyway, he's an excellent dry cleaner and other than a morbid interest in politics he's a very nice man and so I listened to him politely."

"So, you think an interest in politics is morbid? Very interesting…" Mr. Hering excitedly scribbled another note.

"Did I say that? Well, I suppose so. I think anything anyone gets so carried away with that they can't talk about anything else is just not a healthy thing. Don't you agree?"

"I'm sorry, but I'm asking *you* the questions, Mrs. Waldo."

"Oh, is this an interview, Mr. Hering? Are you going to write about me in the paper?"

"Well, yes I –."

"Excellent! Would you also mention that the Charitable Ladies' Association is having a bake sale at the high school Thursday the nineteenth to benefit the homeless? I'm the chair of the public relations committee and I've been meaning to call you but I've been so busy I –."

"I'm sorry, you need to send that in as a proper press release, and I can't promise anything. I have very little free space." Mr. Hering hated local charitable organizations demanding publicity. He was running a newspaper, not a newsletter. "In any case I'm only interested today in talking to you about your husband's candidacy."

"But the bake sale is for a good cause?"

"I am not in the business of pushing good causes, I'm in the business of reporting The News!"

"How rude you are, Mr. Hering. Good Day." She hung up on him and without another thought went back to cleaning the tub.

"So, she hung up on me. Excellent!" Mr. Hering finished his final note with an elaborate flourish and three exclamation points. He was thrilled to the teeth. This hard-hitting interview had turned out so well, the brilliant article that must inevitably be its result could very well win him an award at next year's Journalists' Guild convention. Life was good.

Full of himself and his future accomplishments, he rang Waldo at the sweet shop again, but Waldo's ancient answering machine BEEP! yapped at him like a guard dog.

"Are you trying to avoid me, Waldo? I warn you, this – this coy ploy," Mr. Hering made a note of the inspired rhyme so he could use it in the story, "this coy ploy of yours will not work. The People will not be denied The News. If you want to be a success in politics you'd better learn that and learn it quick. Call me back. IMMEDIATELY! I have a Deadline to meet!" Of course the deadline was more than half a week away, but Waldo wouldn't necessarily know that. "I have a

Deadline to meet!" It sounded deliciously ominous and made for an effective threat.

"Well, I guess I'd better call the councilor," sighed Mr. Hering. He disliked speaking to the Honorable J. D. Millstone, village councilor for the past twenty-four years. Although Mr. Hering considered himself a very shrewd interviewer – and he was – he had a sneaking suspicion that it was Millstone who actually ran their little interviews. It was unnerving, but Hering was convinced the councilor knew exactly what he was going to be asked and had already figured out what was safest to say. Sometimes he even suspected the councilor actually led him to ask questions Mr. Hering had no intention of asking. So it was that Mr. Hering dialed the councilor's number very reluctantly.

"Councilor Millstone's office, Anna Lisa speaking. May I help you?"

"Hello, Anna Lisa, put me through to old Millstone?"

"Oh, it's you Tibbly-Wiggly!" Mr. Tiberius J. Hering's heart sank. Why did she insist on using that nickname for him, especially in the office? At home in the dark it had a certain charm, but it had absolutely none in the naked light of day.

"I wish you wouldn't call me that. Millstone might hear."

"Oh, he's not in. He's out having lunch with someone – and before you ask, I don't know whom. It could be almost anybody. The phone has been ringing off the hook all day. What's up? He never tells me anything, Berry-Cakes!"

"Please! No nibbly-names in the office." Mr. Hering was beginning to blush. "You know how that embarrasses me," he added in a low, husky voice.

"And excites you," she continued in her own version of a low, husky voice. "I know it excites you, my little love piranha. I do so love exciting you – even on the phone –."

"Please, Anna Lisa! It's not professional!" begged Mr. Hering. He hated it when she made him beg. Mostly he hated how much he loved it. As a Pre-eminent ·Moral Pillar of the Community, he needed to be very careful about enjoying himself. Especially in public and potentially public situations. People wouldn't think it right.

"Oh, everyone is in a foul mood today," whined his girlfriend. Although they had been living together on and off for some three years, they had yet to discuss marriage. Mr. Hering hated being tied down. Well, most of the time he hated being tied down. It was all in how one defined the expression *tied down*. "All right, all right, no nibbly-names. So what's up, Mr. Hering? Someone find out about the secret slush fund?"

"A secret slush fund?! Millstone has a secret slush fund?" Mr. Hering started to scribble furiously. "Why didn't you tell me before?"

"I'm just joking. Don't you have a sense of humor?" Got him, she thought, serves him right for being such a pain sometimes. "No, dear, there's no slush fund – at least none that I know about. Besides, I wouldn't tell you if there was. I like my job and I don't want to lose it. Anyway, what's everyone calling about?"

"You didn't listen in?"

"I keep telling you, I never listen in. It's much easier that way. I've worked for a politician long enough to know it's better not to learn about anything I might have to deny knowing about later on."

"Well, I suppose that makes sense. Anyway, it seems Waldo is going to run against him."

"Waldo?! Don't be silly. Millstone would toast his giblets."

"That's what I think, but everyone is talking about Waldo's candidacy and the consensus seems to be very strongly in Waldo's favor. You know, the right man, the right time. Besides, everyone likes Waldo and they can't stand Millstone."

"Well, just because everyone can't stand him, doesn't mean they won't vote for him when the time –." Anna Lisa cut off abruptly and covered the mouthpiece with her hand. Hering could hear her talking to someone, but not what they were saying.

"Anna Lisa? What's happening? Anna Lisa?!"

"Thank you for calling, Mr. Hering. The councilor just walked in. Hold please and I will connect you."

"My very dear Mr. Hering, what a pleasant surprise! How are you doing this extraordinarily fine day?" The councilor's effusive *bonhomie* gushed through the phone line and washed over Mr. Hering in a rich, numbing wave.

"Just fine," Mr. Hering stammered, "and you? How are you?"

"Fine, considering. Although I must admit I'm a little disappointed…" The councilor paused painfully.

"What about?"

"Surely you know, my dear friend? I thought perhaps that was why you called."

"Well, yes, I –."

"Waldo. You called about my good friend Mr. Waldo, didn't you?"

"You heard, I suppose, that he is planning on running against me. Oh, dear..." The councilor heaved an enormous sigh.

"Well, yes, I –."

"You know, I have always held and will always hold dear Emerson Waldo in the highest of esteem. You can quote me on that. He is undoubtedly a fine, fine man motivated by a true spirit of public service. I wish we had ever so many more such unselfish persons willing to take upon themselves the various public responsibilities of our fine community. I always rejoice in any help anyone is willing to give me in my humble efforts. No, dear Mr. Hering, I am only a little disappointed that Emerson has chosen to run against me and by doing so, force our fine community into choosing between his newfound vigor and my sage experience. It will be a tough choice for the good citizens of our fine village and I do not envy them that choice. If only the dear Mr. Waldo had found some way that we might both happily continue to serve our village, instead of demanding that our village choose between us. Surely that choice will be a hardship on our mutual friends. I just can't understand why my good friend Mr. Waldo seems to wish to inflict that hardship on them. For this is a community of friends, is it not, dear Mr. Hering?"

"Well, yes, I –."

"Yes, I admire Mr. Waldo his newfound energy. I confess I envy him. It calls to mind my early days in the public sector when I was inexperienced and untried, but full of a boundless energy. Ah, that reckless energy of youth – I speak metaphorically of course, my good friend Mr. Waldo is nearly as old as I am – that reckless energy of youth is so enormously useful in helping one through the little, and sometimes not so little mistakes, to which your inexperience inevitably leads you. But surely you of all people appreciate that point, dear Mr. Hering. You've been in the newspaper business a long time and have learned from your mistakes, have you not?"

"Of course you have, as have we all, if we are committed to learning, to growing, to moving forward – while preserving that which is best. As my Great-Grandpa Millstone, the pioneer, used to say – you remember I came from pioneer stock, don't you, Mr. Hering?

"Of course you do, Mr. Hering – always on top of things. Very commendable. As my Great-Grandpa Millstone – he founded this town, you will remember – as he always said, 'if it ain't broke don't fix it.' Don't you agree, Mr. Hering?"

"Well, yes, I –."

"You know, I've served my fellow citizens tirelessly for nearly a quarter of a century. For nearly a quarter of a century, dear Mr. Hering, I've helped shape our thriving community into what it is today. Personally, I have no wish to retire – heaven forbid, I relish the challenges of my office – and yet if it is the wish of the electorate that I abandon my post in midstruggle then surely I must bend to that wish, for I respect the wisdom of the electorate. As do you, dear Mr. Hering."

"Well, yes, I –."

"Of course you do. Yes, I admire Mr. Waldo and my disappointment in him for obliging our fine community to choose between the two of us diminishes only slightly the high regard in which I hold him. He is a fine, fine man. And what a lovely wife! Have you met her?"

"Well, yes, I –."

"Which reminds me. She serves with my wife in our local Charitable Ladies' Association. My wife is its President, as you must surely know?"

"Well, yes, I –."

"Of course you do, you are always so well informed, Mr. Hering. Anyway, my lady wife would not forgive me if I didn't remind you that they were having a bake sale Thursday the nineteenth to benefit the homeless. They're such a fine organization. You are going to give them a little publicity about the event, aren't you?

"Well, yes, I –."

"Excellent. It's such a good cause, don't you think?"

"You'll want to come and take some pictures, won't you? My lady wife has organized a lovely little ceremony to turn over the proceeds to the homeless shelter. She'll be very excited that about her picture appearing in the newspaper. I'd better warn her so she won't be taken by surprise when you show up. She'll want to have her hair done especially. Women are so silly about such things, don't you agree, Mr. Hering? But then you're not married, are you?"

"Well, yes, I – No, NO, I –."

"Thank you so much for calling. Mr. Hering. I always look forward to our little chats. I must run though. I've a thousand things to do. Just like you, eh, Mr. Hering? So you won't forget to mention the bake sale Thursday the nineteenth, it's very important, don't you agree?"

"Well, yes, I–."

"Oh, look at the time! Must run. Thanks again for calling. Call again soon, my dear Mr. Hering!"

Millstone had done it to him again. "Damn, I hate that man," he bellowed at the dial tone. Millstone had even made him promise to publicize that damn bake sale. He hated it when people put words in his mouth. In an increasingly foul mood he called Waldo again, only to hang up on the damn answering machine. He determined to show up on Waldo's doorstep. "I'll show him what happens when you try to hide from the Press!" He took his camera with him, the one with the extra strong flash that everyone complained about. Yes, his was a seriously foul mood.

When he arrived at the brick-faced shop, he found it closed, its cheerful bay windows with the white trim empty of their usual tempting displays of luscious chocolates. Upon closer inspection, Mr. Hering discovered small sign in the right hand corner of the left hand window:

GONE TO THE CITY ON A BUYING TRIP, BACK LATER THIS WEEK WITH WONDERFUL NEW SURPRISES!

Well, that is what he *would have* discovered, had the paper on which the sign was printed not curled up. Instead, all Mr. Hering saw was:

TRIP, BACK LATER THIS WEEK

"How dare he?!" fumed the editor-slash-publisher-slash-reporter. "How dare he leave town in the midst of an important political campaign. How irresponsible and how – how flippant?! How dare he 'Trip back later this Week,' indeed!" Mr. Hering stomped about for several moments, and then had a brilliant idea. He would print a grainy black and white picture of the empty shop windows and run a caption under it to the effect of "Local Sweet Shop Owner Abandons Town In Midst Of Important Political Campaign, Citizens Outraged."

"That'll show him!" he muttered gleefully as he strode over to Waldo's home. After all, Mr. Hering was a citizen and he was outraged and when he reported that Waldo had "abandoned" the town, every other right-thinking citizen would be outraged too. So the caption wasn't the least bit misleading. Mr. Hering, no matter how justifiably angry he was at a particular public personage, always insisted on being fair and balanced. It was a point of *professional* pride.

No one answered the door at the Waldo's neat little cottage. The newspaperman leaned on the bell non-stop for a full ten minutes, allowing for someone who might be indisposed to dispose themselves to answer the door, but to no effect. Apparently, the Waldos were bound and determined to hide from him. Mr. Hering was not amused. He marched back to his office to develop the photo. On the way, he thought to drop by Bill Guthrie's village barbershop to stir up some public opinion he might be able to work into the piece.

•

"Yo, Red, how's the fish wrap biz?" guffawed a power-fully built man who looked like a cross between a bulldog and rhinoceros. His old-fashioned, military-style crew cut didn't improve what looks he had. Not that it would have mattered to him in the least. He reveled in his ugliness. It was practically a point of pride. All right, it *was* a point of pride.

Mr. Hering's heart sank. Farmer Bob was waiting to have his ears lowered.

Without deigning to look at the mountain of flesh in the barber chair, Mr. Hering completed their little greeting ritual. "It's bad enough you shovel manure for a living, Bob, do you have to do it in your spare time as well?" It was a ritual that stretched back for over twenty years.

Mr. Hering and Farmer Bob loathed each other. Had loathed each other from the first day they crossed paths. They loathed each other with a loathing so intense it left all lesser loathings outside in the dust complaining about a lack of atten-tion. When it came to their famous quarrels – and their quar-rels were mightily famous in the village – no one else dared compete. Frankly, given the epic nature of the struggle be-tween Mr. Hering and Farmer Bob, why should they even try? Most folks just tagged on and took sides – a few of the wiser villagers ran in the other direction. But they were very few. The village didn't have a sports franchise, but they did have

Mr. Hering and Farmer Bob and that was more than enough to keep them entertained through the long, cold winter months. Twenty years of it and the battle was still going strong.

"D'you hear that Waldo's running for village council?" asked Mr. Hering of Bill, the barber.

"Yeah, I heard," flinched the barber as he razored the neck in front of him.

"Hey! Careful!" yelped Mr. Flick, the butcher, whose neck it was.

"Sorry," muttered the barber.

"Got an opinion about it?" drawled Mr. Hering.

Bill Guthrie flashed Mr. Hering a wry smile. "I've been a successful barber for thirty-five years. You know as well as I do I wouldn't have stayed in business that long if I expressed an opinion willy-nilly about anything except the weather." He waved his razor at Farmer Bob. "And when I'm working on a farmer like Bob over there or a mailman, you can believe there are times I hold my tongue about the weather. I have no intention of offending either one of you. I want to keep cutting your hair as long as you have any to cut – which in both your cases will be forever. Strong roots, both of you. No, today, I'm fresh out of opinions."

"Chicken!" grinned Farmer Bob.

"You butcher those, dontcha, Bob?" grinned the barber back at him.

"And sell 'em at a hefty profit, Bill!"

"So, Red," Farmer Bob turned his beady little eyes on Mr. Hering. "Old Waldo is running for village council. What do you make of it?" Farmer Bob was not going to permit his troops to sally forth without a clear understanding of the lay of the land.

"Dunno. Just heard about it myself a little while ago." The newspaperman chose his words very carefully around Farmer Bob, for if Mr. Hering tipped his hand too soon, he'd never find out what Farmer Bob really thought.

The thing is once it became clear that *The Herald Sentinel Gazette* had an editorial opinion about something, Farmer Bob would immediately disagree with it, down to the minutest detail. Farmer Bob disagreed with everything Mr. Hering said and did, on principle. If, on the other hand, the Farmer popped off with the occasional opinion - no matter how trivial - the village was just as immediately treated to a scathing editorial ripping it to shreds. Theirs was a relationship that had roared along successfully for twenty years, and sold piles of newspapers for Mr. Hering.

That is not to say that Farmer Bob didn't profit from the relationship as well. He was widely respected amongst a certain crowd for his eagerness to take on Mr. Hering. Of course, the Farmer's partisans were not well-educated, nor were they well-informed – and they were deeply suspicious of everyone and everything but their own small circle of like-minded friends. Normal folk, in other words. They were a deeply passionate lot about what little they knew, or rather believed they knew, and were not the least bit shy about expressing themselves whenever, wherever and as loudly as possible. Nor were they shy with respect to throwing large sums of money about. It was amazing how much money they seemed to have to throw about, considering their endless protestations of abject poverty. This curious anomaly had not passed unnoticed by persons in a position to take advantage. A few years back, Farmer Bob had been offered and had accepted a talk show on the local radio in return for a portion of the commercial proceeds. Not surprisingly, his totally fact-free opinions proved enormously popular and Farmer Bob made himself and the radio station a bundle in advertising revenue. Even cutting into Mr. Hering's bottom line. This rankled the newspaperman perhaps the most and he flatly refused to list Farmer Bob's show on the newspaper's entertainment page. Not that this deliberate omission made any difference. Most of Farmer Bob's fans didn't read *The Herald Sentinel Gazette* thoroughly enough to notice, and if they did notice, they thought it a backhanded tribute to The Farmer's success. Which it was.

What the Farmer's fans did read religiously was *The Herald Sentinel Gazette* editorial page. They believed – as did many of Mr. Hering's partisans, interestingly enough – that The Salvation of Western Civilization could only be attained if each true believer practiced total immersion in its mind-numbing commentary and letters to the editor. Each side was especially excited by the opinions with which it did not agree. These commentaries or letters would be carefully clipped out and pasted onto clean sheets of white paper so that the faithful might more easily fax them back and forth to each other and to Mr. Hering or Farmer Bob. (Neither the internets nor cable had yet to arrive in the village. Next year, was the ever unfulfilled promise.) It was of particular importance that there be enough room for the vitriolic little notes they inevitably scribbled across the bottom of each page. When one of these snippets had been bled utterly dry of its gruesome possibilities, the

faithful would retire it to a neatly labeled manila folder, con-
scientiously file it in one of several large cardboard boxes cus-
tomarily stacked to one side of the water heater in each of their
respective garages. There these mothballed battleships would
quietly drift at anchor, until recalled to action in the service of
some new *cause célèbre*. Years might pass, but on a regular
basis, ill-considered remarks made in the heat of some long
forgotten tirade would be carefully dusted off and floated past
an eager audience of political cognoscenti who would enthusiastically murmur their delight or disapproval.

In short, it was professional wrestling, but with what
passed for Ideas. Nothing was ever solved, but that wasn't the
point. It was all about waging the war. Slam-dunking the other
side. Scoring points your opponents will inevitably and irritably refuse to concede.

"Waldo's candidacy, eh? Well, Red, I've not made my
mind up about it either," announced Farmer Bob with a grim
smile. "Why don't you ask Flick here what he thinks?"

The butcher was stunned. He had come to get his hair cut
not his neck slashed and his business ruined. Farmer Bob was
one of his major suppliers, on the other hand, Mr. Hering handled his advertising. "You say Waldo is running for village
council," he waffled, buying himself a little time to think of a
suitable response.

"What do you think about it?" insisted Mr. Hering.

"You have an opinion, don't you?" insisted Farmer Bob.

Wide-eyed, the butcher gaped at one, then the other, and
then at Bill, the barber, who resolutely refused to meet his
gaze. The butcher swallowed and declared, "I'd like to hear
what Waldo has to say before I make up my mind."

As if on cue, both Farmer Bob and Mr. Hering snorted indignantly. Suddenly realizing they had been caught having exactly the same reaction to Mr. Flick's painstakingly measured response, they blanched – again as one. A doubly ominous silence fell over the little barbershop. The two pillars of political punditry glared at each other across the faded linoleum with venomous horror.

"So, Flick," ventured Bill the Barber on conversational tiptoe, "Will you be wanting some Brylcream™ on that?"

"No, it's just fine the way it is." With shaking fingers, Mr. Flick slipped out his wallet, paid up, and beat a hasty retreat.

"Whoa, Flick, here's your change!"

"Keep it! Gotta run. Got a shipment of sheep's entrails I don't want to miss." Flick was out the door and halfway down the street before the barber finished: "So old Jardine's hungering for the haggis again, is he?"

In the terrifying silence that followed, Bill delicately slid his glance over to his two remaining customers. Their eyes and jaws were locked in mortal combat. You'd have needed a chainsaw to cut the tension. Bill grasped frantically at a conversational straw to break the deadlock.

"Hey, Bob, you like the haggis?" he asked.

"Haggis?" growled Farmer Bob after the word had sunk in.

"Yeah, haggis. You like it?" repeated the barber.

"Hate it. Hate it with a passion." growled the Farmer again, his intense green eyes burning holes in Mr. Hering's corneas.

"Yeah, well, I love haggis." fired back Mr. Hering, his own pale blue eyes as bright as gas jets.

"You would, you're just perverted enough." The Farmer's right hand twitched. Where was his keyboard, he felt an opinion piece coming on.

"What I hate, though," continued the newspaperman with curious expression, "Are earthworm burgers. How about you, Bob? What do you think of earthworm burgers? Like 'em, dontcha?"

Farmer Bob turned a sort of purply-red, the color left by squashed blueberries on his wife's best kitchen towels. Hering had caught him out. Earthworm burgers, indeed!

"Damn you, Red, you wouldn't dare!"

"Wouldn't I?" the newspaperman's self-satisfied smirk was as big as Councilor Millstone's classic royal blue Caddy with the white vinyl top.

Farmer Bob's mind raced, he just couldn't let Hering win this exchange. And in front of Bill, the barber, of all folks! It'd be all over town in a half an hour. With the enthusiasm of a new father changing his baby's first diaper, he played the trump card he'd been hoarding for a year and a half. "No, I don't think you would..." The Farmer took a deep breath and whispered huskily: "...Tibbly-Wiggly."

Mr. Hering's face went as white as the barber's knuckles.

"Gosh, look at the time!" burst in Bill Guthrie heartily. "It's nearly four-thirty -– four-thirty, land sake – and speaking of food, I promised my wife to pick up some groceries for dinner. Groceries, yes. All this talk of food just reminded me. I'm getting so forgetful anymore. Listen, guys, if I don't get at it,

Betty Sue'll kill me. You know how she is. Do you mind? Sorry. Gotta lock up. Four-thirty. How time flies, eh?"

"Right," mumbled Mr. Hering, as he tried to force the blood to return to his face and other portions of his anatomy. "I've got a photo to develop."

"Right," added Farmer Bob, scrupulously unclenching his sphincter muscles at about the same rate as the newspaperman. "I've got a – a –." He thrashed about for a moment. "A radio show to work on."

"You first, Bob." Mr. Hering had beat The Farmer to the door.

"Don't mind if I do." And they were gone. In opposite directions.

Bill collapsed into the closest barber chair and loosened his collar.

"I need a drink. And that's no opinion."

•

By the next afternoon, the whole village was atwitter with the idea of Waldo's candidacy – with the possible exception of old Mr. Carle, Waldo's neighbor. Mr. Carle never went out and never talked to anyone except Petey, the boy who delivered his groceries once a week. And Waldo, upon occasion. A very long time ago Mr. Carle had been quite social – notoriously social one might say – but something had soured him on other people and these days he passed his time all alone, but for the company of hundreds of guinea pigs. Needless to say, his house reeked so, that not even the village's visiting nurse would dare to cross the threshold. Which suited old Mr. Carle just fine. He guarded his privacy like a Victorian maiden guarded her virginity. What it was that changed his view of the world so many years ago was not known and although it was much speculated upon, none of the opinions that were eagerly put forth were considered the least bit definitive.

Mr. Carle notwithstanding, the rest of the village talked about nothing but Waldo's astonishing candidacy. Pesky little opinions popped up left and right, like dandelions in the village green after a summer rain. Some were favorable to his candidacy, some unfavorable, and as soon as one was crushed in discussion another popped up somewhere else. Mostly though, there were questions.

Questions, questions, questions.

What did a sweet shop owner, for god's sake, know about politics? And sewer assessments? And transit grids? What did he really want? Who was he working for? Was he truly independent? Where did he stand on pot-bellied pigs as household pets within the village limits? What did he think of parking meters? Did he support military intervention in Luxembourg? And what about abortion and gay rights and whether the public library should be open as late as eight-thirty on school nights? And who did he think he was anyway?

And what about old Millstone? Was he to be put out to pasture on an instant's notice – after all hadn't he served the village well for twenty-four years? On the other hand, didn't that mean it was time for a change?

And where was Waldo, anyway? His shop was closed and there was a sign in the window saying he wouldn't be back until later in the week. How long had that sign been in the window? Where had he gone? What was he doing that took him away from the village at such an important moment in the campaign? (Mr. Hering was especially pleased when he heard people ask that. It vindicated the caption he'd concocted.)

Yes, everyone had questions and precious few answers.

And as for Mr. Hering, the village's chief inquisitor, he rang Waldo four times every day for three days straight but got no answer, and after that first conversation with Mrs. Waldo, even she didn't pick up. Finally he was forced to give up in frustration. He had to go to press or miss his delivery deadline. Absolutely furious at the Waldos for stonewalling him so successfully, he wrote up his interview with Mrs. Waldo as a series of sensational quotes and included a page and a half of man-in-the-street commentary about Waldo, his business, his candidacy and his wife's grievous lack of fashion sense. In a special sidebar entitled "Unanswered Questions", Mr. Hering listed everything he wanted to ask but couldn't since Waldo was nowhere to be found. Mr. Hering was nothing if not thorough. He'd teach Waldo a lesson he'd never forget.

But where was Waldo?

•

"It takes so little to make you happy," muttered Mrs. Waldo as she watched her husband cheerfully sort through his collection of vintage tiddlywinks to decide where to display his latest acquisitions.

"At least it used to," she clucked mournfully. "Why on earth would you ever consider running for public office? It just doesn't make any sense." She shook her head.

For three days – the entire time they were visiting her sister in the city and shopping for sweet shop supplies and vintage tiddlywinks – in one store and out another – over dinner and whispering in bed at night so her sister couldn't hear the details – Mrs. Waldo had been hashing and re-hashing this one single, solitary subject. After three days, her husband was getting a little tired of explaining himself.

"As I've told you, dear, I don't know if I'm going to do it."

"I can read that face of yours like a book, Emerson Waldo. You're seriously thinking about it. I can tell."

"Maybe."

"Maybe nothing. You're going to do it. You are. Oh, dear, I just don't know what to make of this – this madness – and at your age. Really! You should be ashamed."

"Well, my dearest, it seems I've been called to it. Would you hand me that stack of blue and yellow counters over there?" With a substantial harrumph, Mrs. Waldo did as her husband bade her. But she wouldn't let him change the subject.

"Who's called you? Loretta Kepple and her husband? Please! Stieffel? If they're all so gung-ho about a change in village government, why don't they run for office themselves?"

"I don't know. And now those red, white and blue ones with Wendell Wilkie's face."

Mrs. Waldo peered disdainfully at the counters as she passed them to her husband. "Red, white and blue. Who was Wendell Wilkie? Some sort of politician, I suppose. Honestly!"

Waldo smiled wearily but affectionately at his wife. "I love you, sweetie."

"Yes, yes, I know, but I will not let you sidetrack me."

"Yes, dear." Waldo laid the display tray on the kitchen table and offered his wife his full attention.

"As I was saying, why don't they run for office themselves? Eh?"

"I don't know," he shrugged. "They think I'd do a better job, I guess."

"'You'd do a better job' – what nonsense. You collect vintage tiddlywinks and run a sweet shop, for godsake. What do you know about public policy and the administration thereof? You're such a patsy and a pushover, Emerson Waldo. There's something terribly fishy about this whole affair. I just know they're setting you up. They want you to take the flak for something they're plotting. I don't trust them one single bit. Don't think I don't remember how Loretta Kepple talked me into serving on that horrible bake sale committee with Dottie MacPherson."

"That was years ago, dear."

"Eleven and a half, to be exact, and I haven't forgotten how manipulative that woman can be. President of the Ladies' Progressive Thought Society, indeed. That woman has that husband of hers wrapped around her little finger. I know who runs things in that household, don't you think I don't. It's not right. And it's not Christian."

"Yes, dear." Waldo returned to sorting his tiddlywinks.

"And don't you 'Yes, dear' me. Tell them no, Emerson. Just say no."

Mrs. Waldo pursed her lips and truculently folded her arms over her more than ample bosom. Mr. Waldo realized the time had come for a change of subject.

"How long has Mrs. Millstone been the President of the Charitable Ladies' Association?"

"I don't see what that has to do with anything."

"How long?"

"I see where you are going with this, Emerson Waldo, and I won't have it."

Waldo cocked his head to one side and grinned at his wife.

"Is she any more qualified than you are? I hate to say anything negative or unkind about anyone, but she is not to be compared with my lovely wife for either brains, drive or beauty."

Discomfited and a little embarrassed by his flattery, Mrs. Waldo swatted at her husband's arm. "Stop that. You know you don't mean it."

"I do, honeybunch. And you know it's true. If she weren't married to old Millstone, you'd be the President of the Ladies' Charitable Association – and that's no lie."

"That's as may be."

"Oh, Emerson, I don't know if I'd really want that sort of responsibility anymore." she confessed with a wistful sigh. "Honestly, I'm happy to serve just as Publicity Chair. I don't really need or want anything more than that. And considering the way Mr. Hering treated me the other day, I don't know if I even want to be the Publicity Chair anymore."

A loud thump echoed through the Waldo cottage.

"Speak of the angels, feel the beat of their wings. Or in this case, speak of the Devil and hear the thump of his newspaper."

Testily, Mrs. Waldo pushed herself up and away from the table and marched down the hall to the front door, her endless stream of consciousness bouncing off the walls as she pushed forward.

"One of these days, Emerson Waldo, that paper boy is going to break a window. I just know it. He has no business throwing his papers about like a Hottentot. It's not safe. If I didn't dislike talking to Mr. Hering so much I'd call him up right now and give him a piece of my mind."

As Waldo concentrated on arranging his counters, he heard his wife unlatch the front door and swing it open. He noted the squeak of the screen door.

"I'll oil that when I'm finished with my tiddlywinks, dear."

"Oh, my Lord!" he heard his wife exclaim in surprise. It was followed a moment later by an alarmed "Oh, dear!" and then in close succession by a pained "Oh, no – oh, dear me no!" and a thoroughly horrified "Oh my god!"

Then there was a blood-curdling shriek, a thud and a crash. Waldo jumped up sharply, scattering his tiddlywinks counters all over the kitchen and ran to the front door. It swung there reproachfully in the evening breeze – and the rich red-gold of the sunset spilled through it and over the body of Mrs. Waldo. She lay at his feet, sprawled across the floor as flat as her bed of prize irises after last week's windstorm. His grandmother's best hand-painted ceramic hall lamp glittered in a thousand pieces beside her.

The headlines of *The Herald Sentinel Gazette* fluttered in her unconscious hand: "Candidate's Wife Decries Morbid Interest in Politics" and the even more damning, "Is Waldo's Candidacy As Laughable His Wife Thinks It Is?"

Whether he wanted it or not – whether his wife was prepared for it or not – his candidacy had just begun.

two

Waldo got up very early the next morning and went to the sweet shop to organize the new window display. After re-reading what Mr. Hering had written about him – over a breakfast of dismally cold cereal he'd had to fix himself – after re-reading what had been written about his business, his wife's dress-sense and his possible candidacy, Waldo would have much preferred to stay in bed and pull the covers over his head. Unfortunately, that was precisely what his wife was doing at the moment and she wanted no help from him to do it. Particularly not from him. She had said so in no uncertain terms.

So he rinsed out his breakfast dishes and went to the shop instead.

It had rained the night before and the air was fresh and clean. The sun was shining, the grape and lavender lilacs in his front yard were heavy with bloom and a remarkably melodious chorus of birds was partying away in the tall trees.

Waldo took this all in and shook his head. It may be a beautiful day in the neighborhood, he thought to himself, but then why shouldn't it be? It hadn't been the subject of an embarrassing set of front-page articles in *The Herald Sentinel Gazette*. Furthermore he felt as if those articles had somehow forced him to go through a profound change since last night. It was very disconcerting and Waldo didn't know what to make of it. What the nature of that change was he couldn't quite say – but he was very sure he had changed, and changed not for the better. Or perhaps it *was* for the better? He just didn't know. Still, after strolling for a few blocks in the bright sunshine and fresh air, Waldo's spirits slowly began to lift.

He smiled, as was his custom, at the folks he passed along the way and said good morning. They smiled and greeted him in return, but even so, he became aware of a strange unreality about the process. It was as if he were floating down the street in a sort of bell jar. Not a single person said a word about the article in the paper. For that he thought he was grateful, but it was very odd. Gernerally folks were quite forthcoming about current events. Not today, however. Not one had a thing of substance to say to him and that was simply not normal.

Waldo tried pinching himself – in case it was all a bad dream – but instead of waking up warm and cozy in his bed, hearing his wife puttering about the kitchen, smelling bacon and eggs and fresh-brewed coffee, he stood in the middle of the sidewalk in front of his sweet shop and the back of his hand hurt like the dickens. With a heavy sigh, he unlocked the front door and shambled in.

Soon enough he had the window display just as he wanted it. When he concentrated, it was amazing how quickly he could arrange a window. That, and he'd been doing window displays since he was thirteen and worked for his grandfather. He often thought he could do a display in his sleep, although he never actually dreamed he was doing one.

As he stood behind the counter, waiting for his first customer of the day, he found himself absent-mindedly polishing his great-grandfather's antique silver scales. He was eleven the first time he'd been permitted to polish them all by himself. He had been brought up to be much in awe of his great-grandfather's antique silver scales. It had been thoroughly impressed upon him from a very early age that these scales were a precious heirloom that someday, if he grew up to be a wise and responsible man, he might be permitted to possess – but only in trust for future generations.

The memory of this caused Waldo to heave yet another heavy sigh, for he and his wife had never been blessed with children. Not that they hadn't tried, it simply hadn't worked out that way. Now it was too late – for both of them. Perhaps they should have adopted? He tried not to wonder what would happen to the scales when he decided to retire.

He also tried not to wonder what his grandfather would make of the idea of his running for public office. Grandfather, though a generous and much respected man in the community – one who donated to all the civic causes whether they were fashionable or not – had led a very private life. As Waldo recalled, his grandfather hadn't even advertised the shop, relying solely on word-of-mouth.

"If you have a good product you needn't tout it. It will sell itself," was the old man's pat answer whenever the subject was raised.

•

At ten thirty, his first customer of the day walked through the door. It was the tall, exquisitely upholstered Mrs. Van Penner, ostensibly in search of a present for her good friend Mrs. Trudie.

"It's the fourth anniversary of her accountant's acquittal for tax evasion," she noted breezily. "He'd been framed, you know," she added with a conspiratorial wink

"Oh," replied Waldo, trying very hard not to look embarrassed at her assertion. It's odd, but people will tell their sweet shop owner nearly as much as they tell their hairdresser or bartender. At least it had always been so in *his* sweet shop.

Mrs. Van Penner studied the chocolates on offer very carefully, asking elaborate questions about what was in each confection. Did he know whether such and such an ingredient was organic, organic transitional or "that dratted pesticide-laden garbage?" After much fussing, she decided on a half-pound of whiskey truffles, having been assured that real *Irish* whiskey had been used in their manufacture.

"Mrs. Trudie has an inordinate fondness for the Irish," she proclaimed. "Ever since childhood. Claims to have met Maureen O'Hara at the grand opening of the Egyptian Movie Palace on Third Street."

"Maureen O'Hara? Oh, my!" Out of a dimly remembered adolescence, Waldo's long-buried fantasies rose up into sudden focus. Fortunately, he was standing behind the counter.

"Or Barry Fitzgerald, I don't remember which."

"Ah – yes," he stuttered. The abrupt transposition of the old leprechaun's face for that of the fiery redhead quickly brought Waldo's concentration down to the business at hand: gift wrapping a half-pound of chocolates.

As he fumbled about with the gold foil wrapping paper, Mrs. Van Penner's spirited babble slowly subsided into an ambiguous silence. Waldo wondered if she had read the newspaper last night and was now struggling to find something – anything – to say to him. He certainly didn't know what to say.

For some minutes they stood there without exchanging a word. Finally he completed the fountain of lacy gold ribbon that crowned the package and was his signature. He sat the finished presentation on the counter in front of her.

She asked what she owed him, he told her and she paid it without a question.

Then she looked him squarely in the eye. "I read the paper last night."

Waldo's heart sank.

"Tiberius Hering is an ass. And so is Josiah Millstone. If you're going to run against him, you have my unqualified support." Whereupon she handed him a check made out to THE COMMITTEE TO ELECT MR. WALDO. It sported a startling number of zeros. Waldo was speechless.

"*Quis celeriter dat, bis dat,*" she announced firmly. "Who gives quickly, gives doubly." She had gone to Catholic school as a young girl and had retained much of the Latin taught her by the sisters, if little else.

With an opulent sniff, she picked up the tastefully wrapped present for Mrs. Trudie, pivoted on her elegant heel and marched to the front door.

"Thank you," stammered Waldo, "but I –." He was about to tell her he hadn't really decided to run when she cut him off.

"No, Mr. Waldo, don't thank me. Just beat the pants off that bastard Millstone. Whup his ass like it has never been whupped before," she insisted with an uncharacteristic use of the colloquial. Her pattern of speech was usually quite grand. "Good luck and good-bye!"

The door clicked shut behind her.

Waldo sat down in shock. He looked at the check and counted all the zeros twice. He had just received his first contribution, and he'd not even decided to run.

"Oh, dear," he muttered. "What to do?"

He called his wife to tell her what had happened and ask her advice – but she refused to pick up. Her head was probably still buried under the covers. That wasn't surprising. Mr. Hering's remarks about her fashion sense had been frightfully cutting, albeit somewhat accurate.

Although he loved his wife dearly, Waldo had to admit what Mr. Hering had said about her choice in hats was true – and yet, as his mother used to say, "There is only so much truth a person can handle at any one time – and if saying something isn't going to help, keep still."

Clearly Waldo's mother would never have made a successful journalist. But she made wonderful apple pies and had no end of good and loyal friends.

Waldo thought it a fair exchange.

But the question remained: what to do with this check?

He locked the front door, pulled down the shades and called Dr. and Mrs. Kepple.

●

"You don't have to say 'yes,' just to talk to the political consultant. This is a big step for you, you should think about it very carefully." said Mrs. Kepple over a cup of hot sweet tea. Doctor Kepple sat silently beside her and smiled encouragingly.

"I don't know. My wife isn't very happy right now." Waldo suppressed a shudder at the memory of his wife's parting remarks to him that morning from under the covers. Where had she learned such words? He always suspected his wife of unplumbed depths – but who could have imagined that those depths contained such a salty vocabulary?

"That's understandable after what Mr. Hering did to her in the paper. He's a dreadful man. But still, she shouldn't have said the things she said to him. He was bound to misinterpret them. It's his job, after all. Honestly, she has only herself to blame."

"Well, maybe, but she never asked for any of this. And for that matter, neither have I."

"Exactly. That's what makes it so – so perfect. You are the perfectly disinterested candidate. Just what we need. You've no ax to grind, no agenda except honesty and integrity. Can't you see the beauty of it?" Mrs. Kepple was an impassioned and persuasive speaker. "The village desperately needs someone like you to clean things up. Even Mrs. Van Penner sees that."

"I just don't know..."

"Of course you don't. And you're not the kind of a man who makes up his mind just like that!" When Mrs. Kepple snapped her fingers, Waldo jumped.

"You consider things, Waldo. You're precisely the kind of man who should be in office. You know what I said to my husband the day after you said 'You know, Mrs. Kepple, it's all a question of good neighborliness. When it comes to politics, why do we seem to forget that? It's cooperation, not conflict, that makes a community.' – do you know what I said?"

"No, Mrs. Kepple, what did you say?" Waldo braced himself for the worst.

"I said, 'Why must we always vote for quote hardheaded pragmatists unquote and mealy-mouthed panderers? Just for once I'd like to vote for a nice man, a *gentle* man, a man whose heart was in the right place. Someone I could trust implicitly to do the decent thing.' That's what I said. And I meant it."

"Mrs. Kepple, you're very kind – but please, I don't think I'm –."

"I trust you, Mr. Waldo, implicitly. Whatever you decide to do, I trust you. Because I know you'll do the right thing. Not a shred of doubt in my mind. I can't tell you how confident I am that you'll do the right thing. You're a good man, Emerson – I may call you Emerson, mayn't I? – you're a *gentle* man, a man whose heart – truly – is in the right place."

"Mrs. Kepple – I –." Waldo was starting to blush.

"Loretta, please!" she insisted.

"Oh, dear!"

"I won't say another word. Herbert!" She shot her husband a significant look and he moved in for the kill.

"Listen, I'll pick you up tomorrow morning at eight-thirty to drive into the city. Stieffel will come with us and we'll just talk to the political consultant. Just talk. Nothing more. All right? Everyone understands you'll be making no firm commitment by talking to him. We've rented a room at the Hotel Imperial so we can meet in private. And we've booked a table at the finest restaurant in the city to celebrate. It'll be an adventure. You'll love it. What do you say, Waldo?"

"Yes, Waldo, what do you say?" added his wife. They made an excellent tag team.

Waldo gave in and nodded shyly.

He was beginning to wonder if the celebrated Hand of Fate was in all this?

•

"I don't know you anymore, Emerson Waldo!" Waldo had never seen Mrs. Waldo so upset.

"I don't think I really want to run, but they've all asked so nicely, I think it's only polite I should consider their request. Shouldn't I? Hmm? And then there's Mrs. Van Penner's generous contribution. What do you say, honeybunch?"

"Consider it? Consider it? After what the paper's just put you through? After what the paper's just put *me* through? I've never been so hurt and embarrassed in all my life. I'll never be able to speak to poor Mr. Waldorf again – and he's the only dry cleaner in the village! Where will I go to get my dry cleaning done? Have you thought of that, Emerson Waldo? Of course not, your head has been stuffed full to bursting with wild dreams of political power. It's madness. Next you'll be running for President or some such nonsense. How could you even consider considering it after all you've put me through so far? You're frightening me, Emerson Waldo. Frankly, I don't know who you are anymore." She took a deep breath and launched into the home stretch. "I'm leaving you until you come to your senses. I – I just don't know who you are anymore!" With that she burst into tears, grabbed her bags and rushed out the front door and into the car. "I'm leaving the car at the train station!" And with that she was gone.

Waldo wondered if he shouldn't run after her, but he didn't know what to say. To be fair he could see her point. If only she took the time to appreciate his. He heaved an enormous sigh – one of all too many he found himself heaving recently – and decided that after a few days at her sister's, she would calm down and come home. Well, that was his hope. He looked at the clock on the wall and realized he had better get dressed. Dr. Kepple would be by any minute to pick him up.

•

At precisely two, there was a quiet, understated knock at the door of the hotel room. Dr. Kepple rushed to open it. There stood a short, dapper man in a dark blue suit. He was carrying a discreetly unobtrusive portfolio in dark burgundy leather. "Citizens for Waldo, I presume?"

"Ah, Mr. Hegge, I presume." The dentist stepped back to allow the political consultant to enter. They shook hands in a crisp, let's-get-down-to-business manner.

"It rhymes with 'egg', not 'edge', thank you very much."

"I'm sorry, I didn't –."

"Common mistake." Mr. Hegge adjusted his tie irritably and moved into the center of the room. His was a bland, unremarkable exterior with the exception of his eyes. They constantly flicked about the room and its occupants, taking in all the little details that could give him control over whatever situation might develop.

"Hi, the name's Stieffel. I'm a mortician. You can imagine what I have to put up with!" The mortician laughed cheerfully. Mr. Hegge simply glanced at him and hmmed.

"So when does the clock start?" laughed the mortician slightly less cheerfully.

"It started the moment I walked into the room. Shall we get to it?" Mr. Hegge lifted a single, implacable eyebrow.

Mr. Stieffel and Dr. Kepple glanced at each other and nodded hastily. Waldo blinked noncommittally.

"Which one of you is the candidate? You?" Mr. Hegge pointed to the dentist.

"Oh, no. Not me. No, Mr. Waldo here is the candidate." The dentist pushed Waldo towards the political consultant.

"Nice to meet you," said Waldo as he shook Mr. Hegge's hand.

"It's worse than I thought." Mr. Hegge shuddered dismally as he surveyed the candidate. "First of all, get him three dark blue wool suits – less padding in the shoulders than what he's wearing, three flag pins for the lapels of same, a dozen white 100% cotton shirts with a spread collar – oh and two pale blue ones for the rolled-up shirt-sleeve shots – and a dozen red ties in varied but muted designs. Who's taking notes?"

Mr. Stieffel fumbled in his pockets and pulled out a notepad. The dentist fumbled about and produced a pen.

"No vests. No jewelry, except a watch. Let me see your watch." Waldo raised his wrist. "It's a small village, right?" The dentist and the mortician nodded eagerly. "Then it'll do." The dentist and the mortician nodded again. "Just barely."

"Hair is fine. What there is of it. Glasses have got to go. When was the last time you changed frames?"

"Well –."

"My point exactly. I'll arrange an appointment with my optician. He'll fix you up properly. Something up-to-date, but conservative. He's got exactly what you need. Shake my hand again." Waldo did as he was told. The consultant hmmed even more bleakly, then suddenly grabbed Waldo's left hand and turned it over.

"No wedding band? You're not a bachelor, are you?" Mr. Hegge glared at Waldo suspiciously. He took a dim view of bachelor candidates. Of course they weren't as bad as single women, but bad enough.

"No, no, I'm happily married." Then Waldo remembered the scene he had that very morning with his wife. "Well, I was. No, I'm sure I am. Still am. She'll come around."

"They rarely do. Does she drink?"

"No, I don't believe so," interrupted the mortician before Waldo had a chance to answer.

"Damn. It's always useful with disgruntled spouses." Mr. Hegge scrunched his forehead and rubbed it tensely with his left hand. "Are you sure she doesn't drink?"

"No, never," insisted Waldo, who felt it was his responsibility, not Mr. Stieffel's, to answer for Mrs. Waldo's drinking. Or not drinking, as it were.

"Ah, well, if worst comes worst, it still won't stop us leaking that she does."

"But everyone knows she doesn't drink," added the dentist anxiously.

"Everyone," declared Waldo. Why did the little man in the dark blue suit make him want to feel sorry that Mrs. Waldo didn't drink? And what did it have to do with his being village councilor? It was most perplexing. The meeting had clearly taken a very bizarre turn.

"Ah, a secret drinker. We can work with that. A whiff of tragedy surrounding a campaign is always worth a few votes, although a lush for a spouse has to be handled very delicately. What if folks come to blame the spouse's drinking on the candidate? Much better the wife have a serious illness – some sort of fashionable cancer, for example. Imagine her bravely standing by her man during photo ops. Great stuff. No, if she's just a drinker, best to get her out of town entirely. Does she have a dying relative or something? Never mind, but make a note. What was your name again?"

"Stieffel."

"Right. And you're –."

"Kepple. Dr. Kepple?"

"Right."

"Would you care to sit down, Mr. Hegge?" Carefully pronouncing the name correctly, the dentist indicated a sofa and a pair of wing-back chairs near the window.

"Thanks," Mr. Hegge took up the dentist's offer. "Candidate needs to stiffen up the handshake. Nothing new there. That's always a problem with first-time candidates. Also, his personal presentation is a bit wimpy. Needs to practice being firm, but not pushy. Drop your pitch a tone or three. Content be damned, presentation is everything these days. Don't worry, I'm running a seminar for CEOs next weekend on presentation. I think we can fit you in."

"CEOs?" asked the dentist.

"They have the same problems with presentation that politicians have. The only difference is that they have money to spend on the remodel." For the first time, the consultant laughed. It was not infectious.

"Has he announced?" he demanded.

"Announced?" Waldo looked at the dentist.

"Oh, you mean – *announced*!" The dentist looked at the mortician.

"Well, not exactly, but the whole town knows." The mortician looked at the consultant.

The consultant looked at all of them. Sternly. "What the whole town knows or doesn't know at this particular moment is irrelevant. That's why you've hired me. Has the candidate formally announced?"

"No. And I'm still not sure I will," is what Mr. Hegge would have heard had he not cut Waldo off after, "No. And – "

"Excellent." He slipped a sheaf of papers out of the studiously restrained burgundy leather portfolio that lay beside him on the sofa. "Here's your press release. It needs to be re-typed with your name filled in." He waved his fingers across the page imperiously before handing it to the dentist. Then he handed a different sheet to Waldo. "And here's your speech. Memorize it. We can personalize it later, if I deem it necessary."

"Memorize it?" Waldo hadn't memorized anything in years. He wasn't sure he could anymore.

"Memorize it. I don't do candidates who work from note cards. You look terrible shuffling the damn things. Just because you're a stiff is no reason to look like one, isn't that right, Mr. Mortician? Costs votes. Running for office is your sole responsibility now, so take it seriously." He glared again at Waldo severely before pulling a stack of papers out of the burgundy leather portfolio.

"Which one of you is the campaign manager?" he growled as he sorted through the papers.

"Well, I –." started the dentist, looking at Mr. Stieffel uncertainly. Mr. Stieffel shrugged.

"Right." Mr. Hegge handed the dentist two thirds of the stack. Even so, it was a daunting stack. "This is a questionnaire you need to fill out and return to me by tomorrow, express mail. I gather you folks still don't have internet?"

"They say it's coming next year!" offered Stieffel. "What if Waldo were to take a position in favor of –?"

Mr. Hegge cut the mortician off. "Don't open that can of worms. Oh, and when you express that packet back to me, include a full bio and résumé of the candidate." He scowled at Waldo. "For what it's worth." Mr. Hegge clearly took no pleasure in Waldo's candidacy. "Your answers will provide the details I'll use to personalize the print materials and the sound bites for the campaign. Of course, there will be certain givens. He's opposed to taxes, but in favor of revenue enhancement. Opposed to special interest groups, but in favor of access. Opposed to governmental interference, but in favor of law and order. Opposed to pollution, but in favor of industry. The usuals. Oh, and I think you mentioned he was going to run as the 'reform' candidate?"

"Well, yes, actually –."

"So we're opposed to the status quo and in favor of new ideas. In contrast, of course," he continued with another neat little laugh, "to being opposed to inexperience and being in favor of the tried and true." Mr. Hegge shook his head grimly. "Definitely needs new frames." He zipped up his portfolio decisively. "Right."

"This is all very encouraging," burbled the mortician. "I'm certainly very encouraged. You really know your stuff, Mr. Hegge!"

Waldo, on the other hand, was not in the least encouraged, but he said nothing.

The consultant consulted his watch and announced, "Look at the time. Must run. But first, let me conclude with a few pieces of general advice for the candidate. Take notes, Stieffel."

"Right!" Mr. Stieffel eagerly turned over a new sheet on the notepad.

"If you want to be a success, not only in politics, but in the world at large, these are your ground rules: Never do anything you can't successfully deny having done. Or more to the point, never appear to do anything you can't successfully deny having done. You see, no one ever cares what you really do. Their only interest is in what they can credit you with doing. Positively or negatively."

"It's one thing not to do something, but not to appear to do something?" Waldo shook his head. "That's asking quite a lot."

"It isn't that difficult actually. It's rather like a good chess player thinking several moves ahead. If you train yourself to think that way – you do, eventually. Never forget, no action goes unpunished. This is particularly true in local politics. Strive to appear busy, but never allow anyone to catch you actually doing something."

"Sounds like old Millstone," snorted the dentist.

"And how long has he been in office?" demanded Mr. Hegge.

"Nearly a quarter of a century," muttered the dentist gloomily. "I take your point."

Mr. Hegge turned to Waldo again. "If you really must, take credit for innocuous things, but be very careful about even that. Who's to say what is innocuous? Neither you nor I, only the media and its wholly owned subsidiary, public opinion. Or is the other way around, I forget?" he smiled oddly. "Anyway, over the pair of them we have very little control."

"They seem to have very little control over themselves," mumbled Waldo none too amiably.

"Do they now? Perhaps. Which brings me to my second point: Never say anything you can't successfully deny having said. Words are weapons, never arm your enemies at your own expense. And finally: Raise money. Great steaming pots of cash. You can't run a campaign for dogcatcher these days without the big bucks."

"Look at this!" cried Dr. Kepple proudly showing off Mrs. Van Penner's exceedingly generous check. The one with all those zeros.

The consultant sniffed. "Spit in the ocean. Barely covers my fee so far. You want to win this race, you raise money. End of story."

Mr. Hegge stood up.

"Right. I'm off now. I've an appointment all the way across the city in an hour. If I leave now, I'll just beat the traffic. I'll be sending you the bill for the rest of my retainer tomorrow. As you know, I'm always paid in full up front." Then he mentioned a figure that made Mrs. Van Penner's generous contribution pale in comparison.

"Right," gulped Dr. Kepple.

"Right," stammered Mr. Stieffel.

Waldo said nothing.

The consultant shook hands briskly with all, then disappeared as quietly and discreetly as he had arrived.

"Isn't he wonderful?" gushed the dentist tentatively.

"So what do you think, Waldo? " gushed the mortician a tad more enthusiastically.

"I think this is all a terrible mistake." And with that, Waldo left the room. Running for his life.

•

Waldo didn't stop running until he hit his front porch. Of course he didn't actually run the whole way, part of the way he took a taxi, part of the way the train, and eventually drove his own car the last little bit from the train station in the village. But inside where it really mattered, he hadn't stopped running.

Only his porch light was on, the rest of his house was dark. That didn't mean anything – it was on a timer. He stood on his front porch for some moments and stared at the house key in his hand. He had been running like mad to get home, but now that he was home, he was afraid to go inside. Afraid of what he might find. Or rather, whom he might not find. Mrs. Waldo had been awfully angry with him that morning. And he really couldn't blame her.

"Waldo for Village Council!" It was a ridiculous idea, and yet… "Waldo for Village Council!" It buzzed about his brain like a hungry mosquito in search of fresh blood. Why shouldn't he serve? Didn't he have a right to have a say in civic matters? Wasn't that the point of Democracy? Besides, if the electorate didn't want him to serve, they simply wouldn't vote for him. That was all there was to it.

Wasn't it?

•

"Gladys says I've been too hard on you. That it's not your fault."

Waldo pried an eye open and peered at the bedside clock. It was two thirty-one in the a.m. The voice on the other end of the phone line seemed to be Mrs. Waldo and she was crying.

"Gladys says I should give you another chance. She says if they want you to run for office – and you want to run for office – you should run for office."

Waldo was suddenly very wide-awake.

"I'm sorry, but your sister said what?"

"She said if they want you to run for office – and you want to run for office – you should run for office."

Waldo sat up as the words sank in.

"But what do you want me to do, honeybunch?"

"What I want isn't important," she sniffed.

"It is to me!" insisted Waldo.

His wife sat the receiver down and blew her nose. Then she picked it back up and continued.

"I want our old life back, Emerson. I want to take my dry cleaning to Mr. Waldorf. I want to wear big old floppy hats with crocheted flowers. I want to be invisible. But Gladys says all that's gone. I'm a celebrity now and so are you. I might just as well resign myself to this 'brave new world' and make what I can of it."

"Gladys said that?"

"She did."

"Doesn't sound like Gladys."

"That's what I said, then she showed me Arthur's reading list for the English Lit class he's taking at the university. A book called Brave New World was on it."

"Has she read it?"

"Heavens no. Gladys only reads murder mysteries. She just liked the sound of the title and remembered it.

"I see."

There was an uncomfortable pause while they both cast about for something to say.

"Have you read it, Emerson?" asked Mrs. Waldo at last.

"No," he replied, grateful for an opportunity to continue the conversation. "It sounds like a thick book. I'm afraid I've never had much patience with thick books."

"Me neither," agreed Mrs. Waldo. "Gladys tells me all the books Arthur reads these days are very thick."

"Oh, dear!" said Waldo, genuinely dismayed.

"I know," sighed his wife. "And he was such a happy-go-lucky child?!" she added wistfully.

Waldo shook his head at the idea of rambunctious little Arthur with his toy trucks and salamanders growing up to read thick books. Miles away in her sister's guest bedroom in the city, Mrs. Waldo shook her head as well.

After another pause, this one much less uncomfortable, Waldo said softly, "Well, the thing is, honeybunch, I've thought about it a lot and I've decided I can't and, more importantly, I won't run for office without your support."

There was a long silence at the other end of the phone line.

"Honeybunch? Are you still there?"

"I hear you, Emerson."

"Well?"

"All right," said a very small voice. "You have my support."

•

On Saturday night, Waldo officially announced his candidacy at wine-and-cheese event organized by Dr. and Mrs. Kepple at their expensively appointed home on the outskirts of the village. Although it had been put together on very short notice, the event was packed. Even Mrs. Waldo's sister, her husband and young Arthur drove in from the city that afternoon in a show of family solidarity. Waldo was grateful for that. An understandably apprehensive Mrs. Waldo was even more grateful.

Everyone who was anyone in the village was there - except of course for Councilor Millstone and his wife – and Mr. Waldorf. Flick the butcher and his wife, Lorna Jean, were among the first to arrive. She taught elementary school and immediately buttonholed Waldo about increasing the funding for some sort of after school program she was involved with. He wasn't quite sure what the program was intended to do, but he made encouraging noises and a mental note to ask Dr. and Mrs. Kepple or Mr. Stieffel if they knew anything about it.

Bill, the barber, dropped in late with his lovely wife Betty Sue. They were always behind schedule for big events in the village. She ran the only beauty salon for miles around and, as such, did everyone's hair. By the time Betty Sue managed to close the doors, run home, grab something to eat, put herself together, and hit the road, the curtain was usually well-risen.

Mr. Windsor, the town banker, showed up with his ex-wife Gigi. They were dating again to the horror of his mother, but to the unabashed delight of the rest of the village gossips.

Old Mrs. Pederson and her husband Lars trundled in with their instruments, an accordion and a fiddle respectively, and played polkas. They stopped only long enough for Waldo to give his speech. A fixture at village political events, only last week they'd performed at a fundraiser for Councilor Millstone. Frankly, they didn't really care where they played, or for whom, just as long as they had the opportunity to play polkas. Playing polkas – and making lutefisk – was their life. To their disappointment, none of the events they played ever took them up on their offers of lutefisk for the snacks table – although it was very good, as lutefisk went.

The social and political coup of the evening was that both Farmer Bob and Mr. Hering were in attendance. The looks they exchanged as they paced about on opposite sides of the room were exceeded in venom only by the look Mrs. Waldo gave Mr. Hering when he first arrived. Fortunately Mr. Hering was so wrapped up in making a big entrance, he didn't notice her glaring at him. Affording Mrs. Waldo's sister a chance to whisper, "Smile, dear. Never let that beastly little man see how much you despise him. Remember Jackie O." Mrs. Waldo's lips contorted themselves into the best imitation of smile she could manage. It was almost believable.

Farmer Bob sidled up to Waldo when Mr. Hering was in the little boy's room. He said with an alarmingly significant wink, "We must talk!" and then disappeared into the crush before Mr. Hering could come back and catch him with Waldo.

Councilors Felcher, Bland, Biggles, Simpson and Tuck made their appearance about an hour into the event. They arrived together in Councilor Tuck's late model BMW sedan.

Upon entering, Councilor Felcher announced in her notoriously piercing squawk – her normal speaking voice could be comfortably heard at a hundred feet, that is to say, it was only at a hundred feet that it could be heard comfortably – she announced that this was "merely a courtesy call."

"To be sure – oh, yes – absolutely – quite, quite!" agreed the other councilors as they pointedly by-passed Waldo's donation basket.

The aptly named Councilor Bland followed up on Councilor Felcher's remark with a lugubrious "Permit me to follow up on Councilor Felcher's remark" and since no one made to stop him – not that he gave them a chance to – he rolled on with, "A courtesy call, yes – for it would be highly improper for us –

"For any of us!" piped up Councilor Biggles eagerly.

"Thank you, Councilor Biggles," continued Councilor Bland with a voice like a tank crushing wildflowers in a summer meadow, "Yes, it would be highly improper for any of us to endorse a candidate in your race, dear Mr. Waldo."

"Either you or our esteemed friend Councilor Millstone," elaborated Councilor Tuck unnecessarily as his colleague paused for breath.

"Not to suggest that Waldo here isn't our esteemed friend, as well," interrupted Councilor Felcher at the top of her ample lungs.

"Quite so – aptly put – goodness, yes – hear, hear!" came the cordial chorus of inevitable agreement.

This was all, of course, entirely for Mr. Hering's benefit. As expected, he was nosing about for anything that might be construed as scandalous. For example, an imperfectly over-heard remark made earlier in the evening by Lorna Jean Flick about her principal's chicken salad recipe was quietly forming the nucleus for an article on "The Crisis of Confidence in Public Education Today!"

Waldo told the councilors he understood their reservations – although he didn't – and thanked them profusely for coming anyway. They thanked him profusely for his invitation - although he hadn't actually invited them – and they each shook his hand with a well-practiced enthusiasm.

Whereupon Councilor Simpson suggested that someone must take a picture of the four of them with Mr. Waldo. "Historic occasion, you know? Is there a photographer anywhere around here?!" she inquired with an innocent smile. The smile of a baby with the dirtiest of dirty diapers.

Mr. Hering trotted into view with his camera, attached his less annoying flash, and irritably snapped the required shot.

Their posing done, the councilors turned their backs on Waldo and headed for the buffet. As they loaded up their plates, Waldo came and asked if Councilor Flothrew was to be expected as well. The councilors rolled their eyes and Councilor Tuck muttered that the woman never went anywhere with the rest of them. "Very solitary person," was Biggles' comment. "A loner," added Bland. "Marches to a different drummer," roared Felcher.

"Oh," replied Waldo. "I didn't know."

"She refuses even to accompany us on our annual retreat," continued a much scandalized Councilor Tuck.

"We get enormous amounts of work done, nevertheless," bellowed Councilor Felcher.

"Dear me, yes – exactly so – indubitably – indeed, indeed!" agreed the others.

"It was in Las Vegas this year," recalled Councilor Biggles with a wistful sigh.

"She refuses to attend the International Association of Villages convention, as well!" Councilor Tuck was warming to the topic.

"It was in the Bahamas last year," Councilor Biggles sighed again even more wistfully.

"She said it was a waste of tax-payer money," hissed Councilor Felcher at an astonishingly low decibel level. For once you could but barely hear her at all, let alone on the other side of the room.

"What was a waste of tax-payer money was that special audit of the Animal Control Shelter she insisted on," growled Councilor Tuck. "Twenty-seven thousand to discover a discrepancy of a dollar fifteen. I say the woman's pathological."

"Not only that," added Councilor Simpson, "but she –."

"Ahem...?"

Councilor Bland nodded discreetly in the direction of Mr. Hering who had returned from putting his camera away.

As he joined them, the councilors discovered they had nothing more to say about Councilor Flothrew, and instead, to annoy the newspaperman, they waxed poetic about the weather and Mrs. Kepple's extraordinary deviled eggs.

"Only a hint of paprika, you say?" asked Councilor Simpson repeatedly.

"I believe so," answered Councilor Biggles each time with an increasingly fatuous grin.

Presently, Mr. Stieffel stepped forward, clinked a goblet several times with a silver oyster fork until the room settled down. He introduced Dr. Kepple, who introduced the guest of honor.

Waldo stood up and blinked, thanked Dr. and Mrs. Kepple – and Mr. Stieffel – adjusted his new glasses and stumbled as best he could through the campaign speech supplied him by Mr. Hegge.

He was applauded warmly enough when he reached what appeared to be his conclusion, but when his wife spontaneously kissed him in front of everyone it brought the house down. In truth, it wasn't spontaneous, Dr. Kepple had had a quiet word with Mrs. Kepple who had had a quiet word with Gladys who had had a quiet word with her sister.

Dear Mrs. Waldo. Although she'd calmly assured her husband that he had her full support for his candidacy, she was rigid with fear about every aspect of the thing.

And now here she was, in a new blue dress she was convinced made her look like the Hindenburg, in the midst of the elegantly slim Loretta Kepple's damned wine-and-cheese without a clue what to do except grin like a complete idiot. She was grateful beyond belief to her sister for suggesting she kiss Waldo when he finished his little speech.

She and her innards were tied up in one enormous, quivering Gordian Knot of fear about what people were going to say to her this evening. Especially after they had had a few days to stew about what Mr. Hering had said she'd said. What made it worse was that since the article came out no one had as yet said a word about it except her best friend Patty – and all she could bring herself say was, "Well, at least he spelled your name correctly. When I won first prize at the church bazaar for my bran muffins, he spelled my name with an 'O' instead of an 'A'. I was so embarrassed I couldn't go to church for a month!"

But as the evening progressed and person after person made a point of coming up to her and expressing their heartfelt sympathy over what Mr. Hering had written about her and insisting that they didn't believe a word of it, she began to loosen up. Six glasses of Mrs. Kepple's excellent fruit punch didn't hurt either. Mrs. Waldo didn't know it, but her nephew Arthur had spiked it more than once when no one was looking and, consequently, Mrs. Waldo wasn't the only one who found herself loosening up that evening. Farmer Bob and Mr. Hering, for example, nearly came to blows over something to do with wiggly earthworms.

Around eleven o'clock the very giddy and here and there morose crowd finally began to pull themselves together and totter off home. By twelve thirty, only Dr. and Mrs. Kepple, Mr. Stieffel and the Waldos were left.

"I think it was a success," offered Waldo. His wife hiccupped demurely. She excused herself. Waldo sauntered over to the drinks table and poured himself another glass of punch.

"A great success," pronounced Mr. Stieffel as he stretched out in the doctor's favorite chaise.

"An enormous success," muttered Dr. Kepple, eyeing the chaise covetously.

"It's just a start," said Mrs. Kepple, ever the practical one, as she thumbed through the pile of checks in the donation basket. Waldo went and peered over her shoulder as she totted up the numbers. He was surprised to see that those who had given him the least were the ones who had talked at him the most. The handful of big contributors had barely said hello to him. Instead, those contributors spent the entire evening ensconced in the Kepple's gazebo rumbling in low tones to the doctor and Mr. Stieffel.

"What's our next move?" asked Waldo when his wife returned from the little girl's room. He noticed her for the first time this evening. He thought she seemed a little ragged around the edges.

"Go home," said Dr. Kepple. "Get a good night's sleep and tomorrow you start the glad-handing in earnest."

With that, the campaign *officially* began.

three

Mrs. Kepple, as Secretary for Citizens for Waldo (she was also its Treasurer), was in charge of organizing Waldo's week. She had an event scheduled nearly every day for "The Candidate" or "The Candidate and His Wife."

The next morning, however, Waldo and his wife slept in late. Very late. Both of them felt dreadful.

"Must have been something we ate," groaned Waldo.

"Or drank," added Mrs. Waldo, wondering at how fuzzy her tongue had become. What an odd sensation it was, she thought.

On Monday afternoon, Waldo and his wife went to spry old Mrs. Brown's birthday party - she was ninety-nine and had more energy than a roomful of monkeys. Talking with her daughter Catherine, Waldo learned that the old woman had written rather lurid murder mysteries in her youth. He quietly arranged to get one personally autographed and sent it to his wife's sister as a thank-you for helping calm Mrs. Waldo down – although he was smart enough not to call it that.

Mr. Waldorf, the dry cleaner, had also been invited, but when he saw Mrs. Waldo he pointedly got up and left. Waldo caught the look on Mr. Waldorf's face, but fortunately his wife did not. She was in the process of extricating Mrs. Brown's birthday present from her oversize handbag with big red crocheted flowers.

On Tuesday evening, Waldo went on his own to an interesting sports themed barbecue hosted by Mr. Paul in the superbly manicured back terrace of his lovely home overlooking the high school athletics field. The Mission style bungalow was done up in rather high style – all black and white and blue with incongruous little red hearts here and there. Mrs. Waldo had not come along, as it had been intimated that this was a "guys only" event. It was curious, but more than a few of the fellows there did not strike Waldo as particularly athletic. A bit too willowy was his impression. Even the seriously overweight ones were willowy. Still the house was bursting with generously sized pictures of beefy men in various bits of sports attire, so Waldo assumed that Mr. Paul and his friends – some of whom were getting to be quite elderly – had reached the spectator stage in sports participation. Anyway, they applauded his speech with much enthusiasm and then pointedly ignored him the rest of the evening. Nevertheless, he left with a stack of nicely filled donation envelopes. "You never know," he told himself cheerfully.

Wednesday evening was the monthly meeting of the village poodle fanciers club at the community room of Mr. and Mrs. Clark's condominium. Waldo sat politely through the entire meeting, only at the end of which was he recognized by the chair. Then he was obliged to deliver his speech as the ladies dished up dessert in the kitchenette. It was a good dessert. They served a slice of angel food cake with a scoop of vanilla ice cream and a spoonful of fresh strawberries in glass dessert bowls of the color of overcooked lima beans.

Unfortunately when they handed Waldo his, it slipped out of his hand and crashed to the floor. There was a moment of stunned silence while Mr. Clark went pale and clutched at his throat. Apparently the dessert bowl had been highly collectible. Waldo offered to pay for it, but Mrs. Clark glared at her husband and said "Not to worry, he has stacks of them. As far as I'm concerned it's just one less to dust." Still, Waldo knew he'd made a terrible blunder. Mr. Clark shook his hand only grudgingly when Waldo and his wife escaped not long thereafter.

Thursday he spoke at both the village Workers' Roundtable breakfast and village Business Boosters' luncheon. He delivered exactly the same speech to both groups and both groups applauded it equally as enthusiastically.

"Mr. Hegge surely knows how to write a speech," remarked Mr. Stieffel to Waldo on the way to drop him off at the sweet shop.

"I suppose," said Waldo. "But I don't seem to be saying anything in particular in that speech."

"That's the beauty of it. Nothing to offend anyone. The man's a genius. Well worth every penny."

Waldo kept his counsel and said nothing.

Saying nothing seemed to be what was expected of him. Oh, he delivered his campaign speech wherever he went, but afterwards he found himself listening a lot. Several times he tried to express an opinion, but each time his sentences were finished by someone else, who then elaborated on the subject, whatever it was, at length.

Fortunately, Waldo had always been a good listener and soon enough fell into a comfortable conversational stride with what he had always done best – nodding sympathetically and with a smile. Naturally, he was an enormous hit.

Then came Friday.

●

When *The Herald Sentinel Gazette* arrived on Councilor Millstone's desk, he gobbled it up at once. Another big article about Waldo on the front page, and three small related ones. Furthermore, he discovered that Mr. Hering had not deigned to include any of the thoughtful comments the councilor had been making over the last two weeks regarding Waldo's candidacy. Not a single one. What was worse, the councilor's name was mentioned only once in the entire issue, and that only in connection with the Charitable Ladies' Association bake sale: "Mrs. Millstone, wife of Councilor Millstone, blah-blah-blah." And as an added indignity, the article was buried under the obits on page nine. Although the picture of his wife was attractive enough in its way, it was very small and she had already rung him in tears about it.

The councilor was not pleased, not pleased at all. Still, he found the typographical error in the caption under a picture in the article about Waldo rather amusing. He wondered how Mr. Hering was going to dig himself out of that awfully deep pit.

•

Waldo didn't even notice the typographical error. His wife did and so did Mrs. Kepple, but they said nothing. It was such an absurd error anyone with a half a brain wouldn't give it a second thought.

Mrs. Kepple was mostly concerned with Mr. Hering's obvious antipathy towards Waldo. It screamed at the intelligent reader between the lines. Mrs. Kepple had a word to that effect with her husband as she was serving him his favorite dessert: Hazelnut Cheesecake with White Chocolate Ganache.

"Sweetie, take Hering out to lunch."

Dr. Kepple slid a forkful of cheesecake into his eager mouth. "Must I?" he mumbled before swallowing.

"Don't talk with your mouth full. We have to turn Hering around. At least get him to adopt a more neutral tone. For example, the article about Waldo's nephew's unpaid parking ticket?"

"Oh, that. It was just filler. Nothing important." The dentist wondered if his wife would let him have seconds tonight. "Dessert is heavenly, as usual, my dear!"

"Yes, thank you. Did you read the article?"

"Well, no, I –."

"I did. Hering filled it with his usual innuendo about anything and everything. The reader is left with nothing but questions, questions, questions. Why did Waldo's nephew get a parking ticket? Why didn't he pay his ticket when it was due? Why did the university authorities – the ticket was issued by the campus parking patrol – why didn't they follow up on enforcing the ticket in a timely manner? Was there a connection between his nephew's majoring in English Lit and the substantial donation to Waldo's campaign by the President of the village's Teacher's Union? Furthermore, did Waldo know that his nephew's girlfriend's sister's brother-in-law had a criminal record? Etc. Etc."

"Hell, everyone gets parking tickets, Loretta. The nephew's ticket has nothing to do with Waldo."

"Not if Hering decides differently. Waldo's name was mentioned ten times in the article, his nephew's full name appeared only once. Sweetie, it's just the tip of the iceberg if we don't deal with it right away." Mrs. Kepple studied her husband's empty dessert plate.

"Goodness, you finished that awfully quidkly?!" she remarked with an expectant catch in her voice.

"All right, all right, I'll take him to lunch and have a word."

As she served her husband his second slice of Hazelnut Cheesecake with White Chocolate Ganache, Mrs. Kepple thought of mentioning the typographical error to him. He was a dear, sweet man and terribly intelligent, but she had discovered over the years it was best if he didn't have more than one thing to concentrate on at any one time.

She said nothing.

Not that he, she or anyone else could have done anything at this point. The campaign had finally developed a momentum of its own and all anyone could do is hope to hang on for dear life and ride it through 'til the end.

•

Like Mrs. Kepple, Mrs. Waldo was also upset regarding the article about their nephew Arthur's unpaid parking ticket. Unlike Mrs. Kepple however, she was not concerned for what it boded with regard to her husband's candidacy: her distress was much simpler and more straightforward. She was wracked with guilt about the pain the article would cause her nephew and his parents whom she loved very much.

As for the typographical error, Mrs. Waldo didn't give it a second thought – although if she had, her understandably low opinion of Mr. Hering's nature would naturally have slathered a sinister interpretation all over it.

"It's bad enough that horrible little man is determined to hurt and embarrass me in print, but he has absolutely no business dragging poor Arthur into this. Or his girlfriend. Or his girlfriend's sister's brother-in-law. That snide reference to the poor man's criminal record was, in my opinion, nothing short of criminal. Do you know what his crime was? Do you?"

Waldo averred that he didn't.

"Littering."

"Littering?"

"Littering. Well, it amounted to littering. I think they called it vandalism. Something like that anyway. Gladys told me about it ages ago. He's a drummer in a rock and roll band

and was arrested for stapling posters to telephone poles. That may be a nuisance to the telephone company, but Hering made it sound like the boy was a thief or drug dealer!"

"Oh, dear?"

"Tiberius Hering has a lot to answer for!"

"It is pretty awful," agreed Waldo.

"The less you say the better, Emerson Waldo. This is all your fault."

How it could be both Mr. Hering's fault and his fault was a logical inconsistency that, nevertheless, made an enormous amount of sense to Waldo. He determined to take his wife's kind advice and say nothing. Saying nothing these days was his stock in trade as a candidate. He nodded though. Some response seemed appropriate and that seemed the least offensive thing he could do. It appeared to work. Slightly.

A few minutes later an only marginally less aggrieved Mrs. Waldo sniffed loudly. "I'm taking the car and driving into the city to apologize to him personally. And to my poor sister. And to his girlfriend. If she's still his girlfriend. I'm staying the weekend."

"Yes, dear." Waldo tried to give his wife a peck on the cheek as she stomped out the door. She turned her head so he couldn't.

●

When Waldo arrived at his sweet shop the next morning, he found a group of strangers from the city picketing his prem-

ises. Neatly hand-lettered placards proclaimed that they were
from a group calling itself the People's Action Alliance, although some of the placards declared that they were the People's Action Coalition. Yet other placards described them as the
People's Action League and even the Fellowship for People's
Action. Apparently the protesters had failed to find a consensus regarding their name, but they had clearly found a consensus with regard to Waldo. He was to be picketed.

Upon closer examination however, it appeared that things
were not quite so simple. Although the People's Action Alliance was clearly demonstrating against Waldo's sweat shop,
the People's Action Coalition was, in contrast, picketing the
People's Action Alliance. You see, while the Coalition deeply
deplored Waldo's sweat shop, they strongly disagreed with the
Alliance over the use of picketing as a first-strike technique in
confronting exploitative employers. The Coalition preferred
instead a civilized round of negotiation first, then arranging
the all-out demonstrations. The People's Action League, the
third group represented, was there to protest the Coalition.
Why? Because, the League felt that the Coalition's protest of
the Alliance was both inappropriate and tragically divisive –
and ultimately counterproductive to the real issue which was,
of course, to dissuade Waldo from running a sweat shop. And
then there was the Fellowship for People's Action, a tiny but
powerfully vocal group, who had come to protest the League's
protest of the Coalition, for, although they, the Fellowship,
truly deplored Waldo's sweat shop (clearly intimating that the
other groups did not deplore the actual sweat shop as much as
they, the Fellowship, did), they, the Fellowship, had come to
state unequivocally that the League's protest of the Coalition's

protest of the Alliance was in itself divisive and even more inappropriate and tragic than the actions of the Coalition.

Finally, there was a happy jumble of private individuals who simply loved to show up at any sort of protest and sing all the protest songs until the police carted them away. Although to be honest, today these individuals were more than a little peeved that they had to show up so early in the morning. They much preferred the indisputable romance of the traditional candlelight vigil.

All four groups and the various hangers-on had bussed or carpooled themselves from the city in the wee hours of the morning to show their solidarity with the oppressed workers in the village. That they didn't find any did not surprise them, as oppressed workers in villages are often much too afraid or too busy to express themselves in public. That was why the PAA, PAC, PAL and FPA had organized themselves. These were people not afraid of speaking their minds once they had made them up. In the course of a somewhat heated conversation, it emerged that they had, quite understandably, been upset by the caption under a picture in the article about Waldo in the previous night's *Herald Sentinel Gazette*. Waldo did his best to explain that must have been a typographical error, and that they should call Mr. Hering to verify that fact – but several of the angriest demonstrators refused to be cajoled into acting upon that suggestion. Mystified as to what he should do, Waldo innocently asked them what he could do to make them happier. This was a mistake. Naturally, they demanded he shut down the sweat shop immediately and free the workers.

"But how can I shut down what I do not run?" asked a bewildered Waldo.

"Just because you do not interest yourself in the day to day running of your exploitative industry," growled the angriest of the lot, "does not mean you do not bear a personal responsibility for the damage you do to society as a whole in your ruthless pursuit of profit!"

"That's not what I meant," wailed Waldo.

"We're not interested in your feeble attempts to explain away your motives for denying oppressed workers a living wage!" cried another demonstrator.

"But I agree with a living wage?!" blubbed Waldo.

"Then why don't you give them one?" shouted a third.

"Free the oppressed workers!" shouted a fourth.

"But I don't have any oppressed workers?!" Waldo was very nearly in tears.

"Now you deny their existence! How dare you?!" shouted a fifth.

"I don't run a sweat shop, I run a sweet shop! A sweet shop, for God's sake!" Waldo finally began to cry.

"Don't try to wiggle out of it by playing to our sympathy," shouted a sixth. "Admit your guilt! It was clearly reported in *The Herald Sentinel Gazette* that you run a sweat shop. That rag is so virulently anti-union, that for them to have reported on your excesses you must be as guilty as sin of even worse crimes against the worker! Admit your guilt! Admit your guilt!"

"But, but –." but not one more word was heard from Waldo for some minutes, for the demonstrators drowned him out with chants of "Admit Your Guilt!" and "Shut Down Your

Sweat Shop!" and "A Living Wage!" Suddenly someone threw a balloon filled with red paint at Waldo. It missed him but splattered all over his brand new blue and white awning. After that, all hell broke loose. Shouting and pushing and even fisticuffs. Waldo shrank back into the doorway of his shop. Strangely, no one touched him. The demonstrators seemed to be fighting only amongst themselves. And fight they did. Furiously. Venomously. Things did not calm down until Police Chief Gunderson and Elmo, his part-time deputy, arrived. They had been called by a very worried Mr. Flick, the butcher, whose shop was across the street from Waldo's sweet shop. Naturally Mr. Flick was concerned about Waldo's safety, but mostly he was terrified that the crowd might turn on him. For all he knew they might be militant vegetarians as well. He certainly couldn't discount the possibility. Although it was a little nippy out, none the demonstrators was wearing fur.

When Police Chief Gunderson arrived, he calmly climbed out of his police car and told Elmo, who was in the driver's seat, to lean on the horn. A task Elmo performed with much gusto. Elmo loved police work. Perhaps a little too much sometimes. But it worked! The crowd quieted down almost immediately. In the expectant silence, the Chief politely informed the demonstrators that they were disturbing the peace and, after a short pause while they straightened their clothes, shook out their hair and wiped away the blood, the demonstrators politely informed the Chief that they were going to continue to disturb the peace until Waldo shut down his sweat shop. The Chief took a deep breath and politely informed the demonstrators that in such an eventuality he would be forced to arrest them all and, after a affording him a warm and courteous round of applause, the demonstrators politely informed the Chief that that was perfectly fine with them and then, as one, they proceeded to sit down on the sidewalk, the best of friends, and happily sing protest songs in remarkable four-part harmony.

Unfortunately the village was so small the Chief didn't have a jail large enough to accommodate all the demonstrators, so the high school gymnasium was pressed into service for the day, to the great delight of all the high school students who hadn't had such a good time since Billy Ray's Great Dane, Shemp, had followed him to school the previous spring and gave everyone, with the enthusiastic assistance of Maggie Guthrie's Labrador Retriever, Millie, a practical lesson in the facts of life. That is, until Principal Peavey wisely interrupted the presentation with a deftly aimed garden hose.

By the time the last of the demonstrators had been carried away – they had all insisted on resisting arrest by collapsing into dead weight obliging the Chief and his deputy to physically carry them away – Chief Gunderson was nearly ready to be carried away himself. The fifty-five year old career officer had not had such a demanding day since the age of sixteen when he had been sent to his uncle Gustav's farm to shovel hay for an entire summer. Needless to say, the Chief was exceedingly put out and said as much to Mr. Hering, who made careful notes of the chief's remarks.

Mr. Hering also made careful notes of the all remarks made by the demonstrators. He was much too embarrassed to admit that he had made a typographical error in the headline of the night before and decided that it was best to brazen it out by hinting darkly that his sources had informed him of the planned protest far ahead of schedule. His colleagues from the city were much envious of his scoop and remarked on it to him over and over again during the course of the day. Before they had left the city, the demonstrators had dropped off detailed press packets to all the major media outlets and most of the minor ones. They had been very thorough. Naturally, when it became clear that the village police chief was going to arrest the demonstrators, it developed into an enormous story and several reporters and three film crews floated in and out of the village all day long covering the demonstration and its aftermath.

"Hmmm," said Mr. Flick to his neighbor, Bill, the barber, "I think this is what they call 'A Media Circus'."

"Think you're right, Flick," agreed Bill, and they both closed up shop and went down to the Ric's Olde Time Tavern & Juice Bar for a game of darts and a little peace and quiet.

•

When Police Chief Gunderson and Elmo, his part-time deputy, arrived to take matters in hand, Waldo took advantage of the distraction and quickly slipped into his sweet shop, locking the door and pulling down all the window shades.

There he sat down in the middle of his floor in the dark and trembled. He was afraid to leave. On the other hand, he was terrified to stay. Either option seemed equally as bad. Eventually, an inertia born of fear and exhaustion set in and he found himself staying. Every so often someone would knock on the front or back door and rattle the respective doorknob. Each time it sent a cold shiver down Waldo's spine, but he determined not to answer any of those summons. Even when the voice claimed to be Dr. or Mrs. Kepple. How could he be sure it was them and not some protester pretending to be them in order to get him to open the door to face who knew what?

Waldo also refused to answer the phone, which didn't seem as if it would ever stop ringing. As the morning threatened to turn into afternoon, he finally got up and unplugged it.

Eventually, all the uproar came to a standstill. He looked at his watch, the tired, old watch Mr. Hegge had so reluctantly permitted him to continue to wear. It was nearly nine-thirty in the evening. He'd been locked in his shop for over twelve hours. No wonder he was feeling so faint. He had had nothing to eat all day except a few bars of chocolate. He wondered if it was safe to go home now. Then he realized with a start there might be protesters there, as well. Nevertheless, if he went home the back way, through the alleys and through Mr. Carle's backyard and over their mutual fence, he might make it home with a minimum of fuss.

Thank goodness his wife had gone to the city for the weekend. As horrible as all that apologizing to Arthur and company was going to be, at least she had been spared a riot.

Waldo looked at his watch again and decided it really was time to go home.

He got up and stood in front of the front door for a full five minutes before he admitted to himself he was too afraid to open it. The cold shiver down Waldo's spine that would not go away had him convinced someone was still watching out there.

So he turned and slipped out into the back alley, not thinking that it too might be under surveillance. He nearly jumped out of his shoes when a tall, gangly youth with big ears and an older man with a salt-and-pepper beard and a bit of paunch accosted him from out of the shadows near the dumpsters.

"You Waldo, the guy they say's running the sweat shop?" the older man demanded gruffly.

Waldo thought about telling him the truth, then thought again. Then he thought about telling him a lie, but had second thoughts about that, too. Waldo stood there in a confused muddle. The man repeated his question. As if in slow motion, Waldo realized that honesty might not be the best policy, but it was the only one he could countenance. Besides, he was too tired to invent anything.

"I'm Waldo," he stated as flatly as he could. "And I don't run a sweat shop."

The man laughed.

"Hey," he said. "Don't worry, Sandy and me here, we're cool about that. Ain't we, Sandy?"

"Yeah," said Sandy with a goofy grin. "We're cool about that."

The older man continued, "Sandy and me – we decided to come down and let you know we support you." The man came up and patted Waldo on the arm. Waldo thought about edging back into the streetlight, until he realized that that had its dangers as well. Someone else might see him. What to do?

"Thank you," said Waldo as evenly as he could manage. He was unsure what the man really wanted. "Thank you for your support," he added weakly.

"Yeah," volunteered Sandy affably. "We was at Bible Study this evening and we heard about the demonstration and everything and we thought, you know, we ought to come on down and let you know we're behind you all the way." The youth's head bobbed up and down cheerfully.

"That's very kind of you," What was his name? "Sandy. Thank you, Sandy." What did they want, wondered Waldo?

"No need to thank us, sir, like-minded folk gots to stick together, you know?! Says so in the Bible. Ain't that right, Uncle Ralph?" Sandy looked to his uncle, who nodded.

"Like-minded folk?" asked Waldo, worried about what that might mean.

"Yeah, like you and me and Uncle Ralph!" said Sandy.

The older man laughed again, "Don't need to be afeered of admitting the truth around us. We understand."

"I see," said Waldo, not seeing.

"Just one question. You don't have none of them there il-legal immigrants working for you?"

"No, I –." And then the older man cut Waldo off. Like Mr. Hegge. Like Mrs. Kepple. Like her husband. Like Mrs. Van Penner. Like Mr. Hering. Like his own wife. Like everybody else Waldo seemed to have talked to ever since the whole ques-tion of his running for village council came up. Why did no one want to hear him out? They were either for him or against him and it seemed to have nothing to do with anything he said, or rather, with what he didn't get a chance to say. He was be-ginning to feel quite irrelevant to the whole process. Is this what politics is really all about, he wondered? Am I becoming cynical, he asked himself? And shuddered in response.

"See, Sandy, I told you so. He's one of us! I told you so. I don't miss much, no mistake about that!"

"No, you don't, Uncle Ralph – no, you don't!" chipped in Sandy, as he excitedly bounced up and down in his Nikes.

Waldo took a deep breath and continued his interrupted statement. "I don't have anyone working for me. I –."

"Independent contractors. That's the way to do it." Uncle Ralph clapped Waldo on the back heartily . "You're a smart man, Waldo. Gotta be these days! What with all the damn commie trade unionists and liberals trying to ruin what's left of our country. Sweat shops," he snorted. "What bullshit. What a man pays the people who work for him ain't nobody's business but his. You don't like what he offers you, you don't work for him. It's that simple."

So that's it, thought Waldo, out of the frying pan and into the fire. "I'm sorry – Ralph – I'm not sure it is that simple."

"Sure it is. Black and white issue – no pun intended." Sandy and his uncle laughed uproariously. Waldo began to feel a little sick to his stomach. But decided that it was probably due to his not having eaten.

"I'm sorry, I'm on my way home," mumbled Waldo disconsolately.

"Well, don't you worry about them commie socialist nazis bothering you again. Me and the boys have decided to set up an armed guard outside your shop. Twenty-four hours a day. See?" Uncle Ralph pulled Waldo around the corner and discreetly pointed out a flash of gun-metal on the roof of Mr. Flick's butcher shop across the way. Someone had been watching his front door!

"Does Mr. Flick know about this?" asked Waldo in ill-disguised horror.

"Nah, but he won't mind. His wife's my first cousin once removed. It'll be okay. Trust me."

"I have to go home now," repeated Waldo nervously. "I haven't eaten much today. I –."

"You want Sandy to walk you home?" asked Uncle Ralph solicitously. Sandy patted a suspicious bulge under his jacket.

"No!" squeaked Waldo. "No," he managed to say more calmly. "I'll be just fine on my own. Thanks. Thanks for everything." And without waiting for a response, Waldo turned and ran off down the alley, heading for home.

"Excitable guy!" remarked Sandy to his uncle as they shambled off in the other direction.

"Probably eats too much chocolate," replied his uncle placidly as he offered his nephew a pinch of snoose.

•

As Waldo approached his neighborhood, he forced himself to slow down. God forbid the smack of his wing tips against the pavement should catch anyone's attention. There was no point, he realized, in trying to use his front door. Someone was surely watching. Even climbing over his back fence was potentially dangerous – as his experience with Sandy and Sandy's Uncle Ralph had demonstrated.

Waldo cut down Elm Street and through the alley to Chestnut. As he drew near Chestnut, he slowed to a tiptoe. He peeked out carefully from behind a large stand of holly bushes at the corner.

No one was in sight.

He strolled – ambled, really – right up to Mr. Carle's driveway.

No one accosted him.

All the way from the sweet shop Waldo weighed whether or not he should knock on Mr. Carle's front door and ask if he could climb over their mutual back fence, but now that he was here and there appeared to be no lights on inside, he decided the less fuss the better. So he slipped along as quietly as he could past the house and slowly – as painstakingly as if he were mixing a nitroglycerine cocktail – he unlatched the side gate. He managed to get almost halfway across the moonlit backyard before he caught the clitch-clatch of some sort of gun being readied to fire.

"It's just me, Mr. Carle," he whispered, hoping not to alert any protesters that might still be lurking about.

"Turn around, you!"

"I said it's me," he whispered a little louder. "It's Waldo!"

"Waldo?! What the hell are you doing sneaking about my backyard?"

"It's a long story."

"I'm all ears."

•

"You know I once considered entering public life myself, but now I go in for domesticating piranha. So much more civilized." Mr. Carle laughed a brittle laugh.

Waldo frowned. "I thought you raised guinea pigs?"

"I do. It's just that the bit about piranha sounded so much wittier. See, even I'm a fraud. Such is Life." The old man sighed heavily and eased back in his tattered easy chair. "So what did your 'political consultant' say? This has got to be good."

"He criticized how I looked, said terrible things about my wife, handed me empty words to memorize and gave me three pieces of advice."

"And that advice was –?" The old man took off his glasses and rubbed his eyes in anticipation.

"Never appear to do anything you can't successfully deny having done. Never say anything you can't successfully deny having said. And third, raise money. Great steaming pots of cash, he said. It was thoroughly degrading."

"Good, good. The political life is a life of systematized degradation. If you can't tolerate even a small dose of Mr. Hegge," he pointedly pronounced the consultant's name wrong, "you will never survive, let alone prosper. So what bothered you most about what he said?"

"If you have enough money, you can do anything." Waldo mumbled disconsolately. Mr. Carle laughed again.

"Well, of course it's true. Other than certain activities still governed by the laws of physics – if you have enough money, you *can* do anything."

"No, it's not true, old man! There are lots of things you can't do. There are laws against –."

Mr. Carle cut Waldo off sharply. "Laws? Of what importance are Laws? They are of no importance whatsoever, except as a source of revenue for lawyers."

"But surely –."

"Listen to me, boy: There is nothing illegal in this world – nothing."

"I don't understand?"

"What is legal is what a group of lawyers say is legal – and if you have enough money to catch a lawyer's attention, he or she will say absolutely anything you want. You know," added Mr. Carle with a curious snort, "our much touted legal system is merely a complex and highly profitable filtration system –."

"A filtration system?" Waldo didn't follow Mr. Carle's stream of consciousness.

"A filtration system, m'boy! Its sole purpose is to select out the cleverest and most amoral and reward them with as much wealth and power as they can amass. Its sole purpose. Why if the system were not so complex, anyone could get away with what they wanted. Anyone. People like you and me, for example. And that would never do – never, never! No, as it is, only the elect, no pun intended, can have their cake and eat yours, too. No, my boy, Laws exist solely to show the elect how to accomplish the illegal in the most ingenious manner possible. Oh, it's a marvelous and elegant thing to behold! Perhaps humanity's greatest achievement: The Rule of Law." The old man began to laugh so hard, he started to choke.

Waldo ran and got Mr. Carle a glass of water. He hoped the glass was clean, it was in the cupboard. "This is very distressing. I know you are wrong. All wrong. There is such a thing as goodness, and I believe in it. I believe it's important for each of us to try to be good."

"Goodness. Yes. And what do you mean by Goodness?" demanded the old man between gulps of water.

"Doing good deeds."

"And how do you know you are doing a good deed?" Mr. Carle handed him the empty glass for a refill. Waldo bounded to the kitchen as he answered him.

"When you do a good deed, you – well, you feel good!" shouted Waldo in reply.

"Ah, yes, virtue as its own reward, indeed," muttered the old man to himself, then shouted back at Waldo in the kitchen, "And if you don't do that 'good' deed? How do you feel?"

"Well, bad, I suppose. Guilty."

"Guilty. Ah!" Mr. Carle laughed his grim and brittle laugh again. "And what is guilt?" he shouted at Waldo.

Waldo returned to the living room and handed Mr. Carle the glass.

"What is guilt, Waldo?" he asked again, in a disturbingly normal tone of voice.

Waldo shrugged. He didn't have an answer to that question.

The old man snapped at him. "Guilt is the fear you have done something wrong. Do not, in your mad rush for the carrot, my boy, forget the stick that is driving you towards it. Of course, I'm not surprised in the least to hear you arguing on behalf of 'goodness'. YOU are a 'good' person. An extremely 'good' person. A notoriously 'good' person. No doubt this is why the dentist, his wife and the undertaker say they want you to run for office?"

"Well –."

"They're all mad and so are you. 'Good' people have no business in politics. Not only will the other politicos eat you alive, the public won't stand for it."

"The public won't stand for it? Now you have me thoroughly confused. I thought that was the point, the public wants some goodness in –."

"Oh, please! The public will never elevate someone to high office unless they are supremely confident they can look down on him immediately thereafter. The public hates people that are better and more 'moral' than they are. Absolutely despises them. This is particularly true about reform candidates – you're supposed to be The Reform Candidate, right?"

"Yes."

"Listen to me. As a "reformer", you dare not reform a thing. The public, despite what it may shriek to the contrary, simply will not stand for it. But back to this 'goodness' thing."

"What about 'goodness'?"

"Unspeakable amounts of money and effort have been spent to teach us to be 'good' little soldiers, and of course, in your case – and in the case of most people most of the time – it was and is a shrewd investment that has paid off big. You obsess over your damned carrot and refuse to notice the stick. You work like the mother of two-year-old quintuplets to convince yourself that only the carrot exists. All the while burying that damned stick deep within the dark, dank recesses your soul. Where it was designed to be. Where it works best."

"But –."

"This is precisely the way Society and the forces that control Society want you. Why? To incapacitate you. A 'good' person is a weak person. A 'good' person is a person who can be controlled. For there is no 'good' that does not arise from a sound foundation of fear."

"What?!"

"As Oscar Wilde put it so beautifully, 'The terror of society, which is the basis of morals, the terror of God, which is the secret of religion – these are the two things that govern us.'"

"That's horrifying!" blanched Waldo.

"It's horrifyingly true, although slightly less than accurate. He should have said, 'these are the two things that allow us to be governed.' For it is terror and terror alone that permits society to function so efficiently. People who have no fear are people who cannot be controlled. And when people cannot be controlled, society ceases to function. Fortunately, there is no one that doesn't fear *something*. Which is why society continues to function, despite everyone's best efforts." Mr. Carle laughed unpleasantly. "The people who know and understand the fears of others are the people who run the world. Or rather, are the people by whom the world permits itself to be run. For

knowledge is power, and the fear-knowledge is the most pow-
erful knowledge of them all."

Waldo collapsed into a chair, overcome.

"No, dear boy, good behavior counts for nothing in this
world, only fear matters. And money. And plausible deniabil-
ity. That's all. Wake up, my boy! It has always been so, and
will always be so, *in saecula saeculorum*." With that he made
the sign of the cross with his middle finger, and laughed sav-
agely, "Missa est!"

"You've described a world in which I don't think I want to
live. In which I don't think I can live!" wailed Waldo.

"That means one of two things, my friend. Either you are
not the kind of person that should live in this world. Or you
are precisely the kind of person that should live in this world."

"I want to believe in Truth. I want to believe in Justice."

"Of course, you do. I'm not at all surprised. Why, Waldo?
Why do you want to believe in Truth and Justice? Why? Perhaps because deep in your heart you want to believe there is
more truth and justice in your little finger than in all the people who are running circles around you."

"Well, I –."

"Come on, you envy the bastards their success, don't you?
Anyone would."

"No. No, I don't."

"Yes, you do. Oh, stop, if you want to be a success in this
game, you must follow the rules and the most important rule
of all is to dare to break the rest of the rules when it suits you."

Waldo shook his head. "I don't think I have it in me. I
don't think I want to have it in me."

"You've been hobbled, that's for sure. But is that a permanent condition? Of course, it's all up to you. Be happy with your little corner of the paddock, or run away. Of course, they shoot horses that have been too badly damaged. That are of no use. Perhaps you need to be shot."

"What?"

"And then again, perhaps not. But let us examine your Goodness, shall we? You say you believe in Truth? Do you lie?"

Waldo began to well up. The old man pressed him even more brutally.

"Of course you do. It's 'standard operating procedure' in this, the best of all possible worlds. We all lie, Waldo. The basis of polite behavior is untruth. A truthful person is always unwelcome, even amongst the 'good'. Especially amongst the 'good', for they have the most to hide."

"I can't – I don't – I – ?"

"The 'good' fear being found out for what they really are – just as evil and bitterly confused as the rest of us. They are terrified of being proved the vicious little hypocrites they know themselves to be."

"Yours is a very, very cynical view of the world." Waldo hid his tear-stained face behind his fists. "And what's worse, you make it all sound so logical. So right. I can't argue with you. I want to. I want to desperately! But I don't know what to say. I don't know how to say it. Oh, god, I wish I did!"

"I wish you did, too." Waldo looked and found tears streaming down the old man's face as well. "Why do you think I left the world and hid myself in a nest of foul-smelling guinea pigs. It's the only way I could find to survive. And every day I question the value even of that. Give up this mad idea of political power. Go back to your sweet shop and fill the world with fleeting moments of joy and pleasure. It may be all that matters in the end. If anything matters at all. Now go away and leave me alone with my guinea pigs."

•

By the time Waldo finally climbed over the fence and let himself in, he was in a very bad state. He wanted – he needed to talk to his wife, but it was far too late to call her at her sister's – they would all have gone to bed by now. So he made a sandwich instead – by the light of the refrigerator's open door – then ate it in the dark and went to bed himself. He was exhausted – physically, mentally, emotionally and even, he feared, spiritually.

But as Waldo tugged his grandmother's quilted coverlet under his chin, he found he was unable to sleep. What Mr. Carle had said had shaken him to his very core. Was the world really so horrible? Waldo desperately did not want to believe it, and yet –? People in their heart of hearts are good, aren't they? he demanded of himself again and again and again.

Eventually, he managed to squeeze it all into a tiny crack in his brain and plaster it over. He had to. Or he would go mad. Or perhaps it was already too late.

four

At five-thirty in the morning, Waldo was awakened by an insistent ringing. Apparently he'd managed to drop off, after all. Without thinking, his fingers scrabbled for the receiver.

"Hullo?"

"Waldo, is that you?"

It was Mrs. Waldo. She was upset.

"Are you all right? I rang all yesterday evening at the shop and at home. You didn't answer!"

"I'm sorry, I unplugged the phone at the shop. It wouldn't – there was a little disturbance. I didn't get home until very late and then I went straight to bed."

"Little disturbance? LITTLE DISTURBANCE?! It was all over the news here. Reporters even came here to my sister's house demanding a response. We gave them a response all right. We locked the door and turned out the lights. They finally stopped ringing the doorbell at eleven fifteen. And they only stopped because Gladys called the police." Mrs. Waldo paused for a moment. "Oh, Good Lord, I can already see some of them out on the sidewalk this morning! They must have camped there all night?!"

Waldo scrambled out of bed and peered out carefully from behind the blinds. "Gosh! There's a news crew out front here, too!"

"You have to make them go away, Emerson!"

"I'm not sure I know how to. I didn't ask them to come in the first place."

Mrs. Waldo snorted in disgust. "When you decided to run for public office, Emerson Waldo, you gave them permission. Don't you realize that?"

Waldo tore at his hair. "I'll call Dr. and Mrs. Kepple. Maybe they'll have an idea what to do?"

"Loretta Kepple has never been anything but trouble. I blame her for everything."

Waldo peered out the window again. "Oh my, I think another news crew has arrived!"

"Emerson, they won't be satisfied until you go out and talk to them."

"I don't know what to say?"

"To begin with, tell them to leave my sister and her family alone. And Arthur's girlfriend's sister's brother-in-law! They aren't running for office. They shouldn't have to put up with this."

"I'll see what I can do. Tell Gladys I'm sorry. And Arthur. And Henry. How's Henry handling this?"

"It's all Gladys and I can do to keep him from going out there and knocking heads together. Do something, Emerson, and fast!"

With a loud clang, she hung up.

Waldo got up and performed a few necessary ablutions. Then he called the Kepples. They were wide-awake, too.

"Where the hell were you yesterday?" roared Dr. Kepple into the phone. "Do you have any idea what's going on around here?"

"Give me that phone, you idiot," Waldo heard Mrs. Kepple shout at her husband as she wrestled him for the receiver.

"Waldo, Waldo, where are you, Waldo? Are you at home? Are you all right?" she asked, once the receiver was safely in her possession.

"I'm at home, Mrs. Kepple. But I'm far from all right. I thought someone was going to kill me yesterday! What is this all about? It was just a typo. Doesn't anyone understand about typos?"

"Where was he yesterday?" roared Dr. Kepple in the background. His wife waved her hand to shush him.

Waldo went on unabated. "There are two news crews camped outside my house right now – and I just talked to my wife. She's staying with her sister in the city and they've been besieged by reporters as well. ARE besieged – right now!"

"Where is he? Has he told you where he is?" Dr. Kepple continued to roar questions his wife continued to shush.

"What are we going to do, Mrs. Kepple? What? What? What?"

Mrs. Kepple took command. (She would have made an excellent General – or at the very least a Drill Sergeant!)

"First of all, both of you shut up and calm down! Nothing will be solved by hysterics. Secondly, take a deep breath and think about that for a moment. What if the media got a picture of either of you in hysterics? The worst thing you can do in this situation is to appear hysterical. Are you with me?" She turned away from the phone to her husband, "Pookums?"

Waldo heard a disgruntled and carefully muffled, "Yes."

"Emerson?"

"Yes, I'm listening."

"I have one question for you," announced Mrs. Kepple solemnly. "I need you to answer it honestly."

"All right, all right. What is it?"

"Do you run a sweat shop?" was the quietly dropped bombshell.

"Are you insane?" shrieked Waldo, "I thought you –."

Generalissima Kepple snapped Waldo to attention. "Calm down and answer the question!"

"No," he grumbled. "No, of course not."

"Never in your life?" amplified and clarified Mrs. Kepple.

"Never in my life!" shouted Waldo. "I run a god-damned sweet shop. It was a god-damned typo in that god-damned rag of a god-damned newspaper!"

"Calm down, Emerson. Calm down. I had to ask the question. I didn't expect any other answer but the answer you gave me – but I had to ask the question. Do you understand? I had to ask the question. All right, then, this is what we do –."

The Generalissima laid out her strategy clearly and cogently. Then issued everyone their marching orders. All acquiesced without a murmur.

The game was afoot.

•

At promptly eleven-thirty, a poison green BMW pulled up in front of Waldo's residence. Out of the back seat stepped a tall, imposing figure in a dark blue suit. He was wearing mirrored sunglasses. The news crews recognized him, of course, but he ignored them. Well, strictly speaking he didn't ignore them. He simply swatted them away, as someone might swat away an annoying fly or insect. He said not a word, but went directly to Waldo's front door and knocked once. It opened to admit him and only him and then slammed shut.

Ten minutes later, Police Chief Gunderson and his part-time deputy Elmo drove up. They climbed out of the police car in their blue dress uniforms, and limped up to Waldo's front door. (They had yet to recover from the rigors of their arresting experience of the previous day.) They knocked once and the door opened to admit the Chief. Elmo remained on the front porch and glared as fiercely as a bulldog at the reporters. Fortunately, since they were from the city and didn't know him personally, his expression was highly successful in inspiring them to keep their distance.

Five minutes later, the door re-opened and out stepped the imposing figure in the dark blue suit. He was accompanied by shorter figure in another dark blue suit. A figure rather less, but still somewhat imposing. It was Waldo.

Finally, they were joined by a third and final imposing figure in dark blue, Police Chief Gunderson. The Chief had a very grim and pained expression wrapped around his mug. Part of it was professional of course, but most of it was thanks to the fact that he'd dropped his hat inside and when he'd bent to pick it up his back went out on him in a very major way.

The tall man took off his mirrored sunglasses and cleared his throat.

The news crews and various reporters swarmed up to the porch and stuck their cameras and microphones into his face, or rather, as close to his face as they dared. (He had a reputation for dealing promptly, harshly and expensively with reporters who crossed him.)

"My name is Edward Kibble. I am the principal in Kibble, Tomaine and Associates. Our legal reputation speaks for itself. We have never lost a case."

He slipped his mirrored sunglasses into his breast pocket.

"I am here today to speak to you on behalf my client, Emerson Waldo."

Waldo stood up straight and frowned the dour and prodigious frown he'd been practicing in the mirror for the last hour and a half.

"Mr. Waldo has been the victim of a particularly vicious libel. The day before yesterday in *The Herald Sentinel Gazette* it was claimed that my client runs a sweat shop. He most emphatically does not. His reputation has been grievously damaged. Furthermore, his shop was vandalized yesterday in the course of a riot engendered by that libel. He was also, owing to that riot, unable to conduct his normal business and has suffered considerable financial loss. Publication of this libel has also put his person and the persons of his family in danger of suffering grievous bodily harm as well. To speak frankly, ladies and gentlemen of the press, my client, his wife and his family have been put in fear for their very lives."

Police Chief Gunderson shifted his weight from one foot to the other in an attempt to relieve the pain in his lower back. It didn't help. His glower was getting more brutal by the minute. Duty be damned, he was going straight from here to his chiropractor!

"Mr. Waldo has retained my firm to sue *The Herald Sentinel Gazette* for an as-yet-to-be-determined sum. We will, naturally, be suing for defamation of character and for financial losses rising out of the original libel, as well as investigating the possibility of an additional civil suit for damages resulting from an intent to cause bodily harm. I have also been directed to file a full slate of criminal charges with Police Chief Gunderson against *The Herald Sentinel Gazette* for their wholly irresponsible behavior in this matter."

The reporters burst into a sudden cacophony of questions. Mr. Kibble, Esquire raised his elegantly manicured hand for silence. When it had been achieved, he continued in his terrifyingly even tone.

"We will take no questions at this time. Go home. Or better yet, go to the offices of *The Herald Sentinel Gazette* and follow up there on the statement you have received here. Thank you and Good Morning!"

He put his mirrored sunglasses back on and with the two policemen's assistance, herded Waldo into his BMW and drove off.

The reporters turned on the police chief and deluged him with an avalanche of questions. Police Chief Gunderson figured he had a choice: Elmo on the car horn, or Mr. Kibble's approach. To Elmo's disappointment, the Chief raised his hand for silence. To his surprise, it worked.

"Gentlemen – and lady!" The Chief doffed his hat chivalrously, if painfully, in the direction of the rather attractive political reporter for one of the evening news teams, then turned back to the main body of reporters and resumed his off-putting grimace. "You've gotten the only story you're going to get at this location today. I suggest you move along now, before I interest myself in our village's code regarding loitering, public nuisance..." The Chief glared at an inappropriately disposed of disposable coffee cup. "...and littering!"

The reporters exploded into yet another violent cacophony of questions. Police Chief Gunderson raised his hand. The reporters eventually settled down.

"I have nothing more to say to you this morning, except to suggest that if this neighborhood isn't back to its usual Sunday calm in, say..." he consulted his wristwatch, "... ten minutes – I intend to begin a new conversation with each and every one of you – one right after the other – beginning with the following words, 'You are under arrest, you have the right to remain –.'"

It was amazing how quickly they vanished when they saw he was serious. Within five minutes all that was left was two trampled beds of pansies and a row of crocuses that would never stand tall again. At least not this season. The reporters even picked up their ill-disposed disposable coffee cups.

They hadn't given in to his threats, of course. They were each and everyone of them tireless defenders of journalistic freedom! It was merely that, upon reflection, they recognized that The Story wasn't here anymore. It had been very deftly transferred – by the redoubtable Mrs. Kepple in absentia – to the offices of *The Herald Sentinel Gazette*. Like the rats they were, they rushed off at the first hint of a properly paid piping.

"Gee, sir, maybe we oughta drive over to the newspaper?" wondered Elmo with an unhealthy excitement rising in his voice. "I'll bet them reporters are all heading over there right now. Mr. Hering'll need some help with the crowd control end of things."

Despite the pain in his lower back that was screaming for the nimble hands of his chiropractor, Police Chief Gunderson smiled.

"Yep, Elmo, I dare say he could use a little help. But, you know, I figure he's more'n earned his little crowd control problem. Drive me to my chiropractor instead. Slowly. No fast corners like on our way over here."

"Yes, sir! No, sir! Sorry, sir!"

"Now help me into this damned car. I can barely move!"

•

"Yo! Hering! How's it danglin'?" the voice crackled and wandered in and out of phase.

"My participle is danglin' just fine. God, I hate it when you call me on your damned cell. You gotta sign up for a better service. What do you want, Williams?" Mr. Hering saved the document he was working on and leaned back in his chair and stretched luxuriously. Williams, with whom he had gone to university and with whom he had maintained a friendship over the years, was a talker. Mr. Hering settled in for one of their long Sunday morning chats.

"A scoop."

"And what concern of mine is that?" laughed Hering.

"You're the scoop, babe."

"Excuse me?" Mr. Hering continued to laugh.

"You're the scoop. Right at this very minute three film crews and a whole herd of print hacks (myself included) are heading over to your office and if you don't want to face us, you'd better hightail it out of there."

As if to underscore the urgency of his friend's suggestion, Mr. Hering's phone lines suddenly all lit up. Mind you he had only two lines and he was on one at the moment, but it was still impressive, if only in a symbolic sense.

"Shit! What's up?" Hering bolted upright in his chair.

"I tell you – you give me the exclusive. That's the deal."

Hering knew if there really were a problem, Williams would treat him as well as he could dare hope for. What with the news biz being as cut-throat as it was, it wasn't much, but it was something.

"Done. What's up?"

"You're about to be sued. Big time."

"Yeah? What for?" blustered Mr. Hering heroically. The newspaperman knew he was potentially, as they say in the libel attorney racket, "exposed" on a number of fronts. Given the riot yesterday in front of Waldo's sweet shop, however, Mr. Hering had a pretty good idea what the problem was likely to be. His innards did a major flip-flop. "Exposed" didn't even begin to describe how naked and defenseless he was on the point he feared Williams was about to relate to him.

Williams did not disappoint him. Mr. Tiberius J. Hering went white in the face and very nearly brown in the pants.

"Intent to commit bodily harm too?"

"That's what he said."

"Well, that's patently absurd."

"You on the record?"

For a brief moment, Mr. Hering had forgotten he was not speaking a friend, but to fellow newspaperman.

"Uh," he thought fast, "Yeah. Yeah, that's on the record. Attribute it to 'sources close to management.'"

"You're the only employee, Hering. Won't wash."

The publisher-slash-editor-slash-reporter-slash-photographer-slash-typesetter frowned. "Right. Attribute it to 'friends of' –."

"I have another scoop for you. Other than me, you have no friends right now."

"All right, all right, goddammit, attribute it to me."

"Thanks. What else do you have to say?"

Mr. Hering took a deep breath and intoned sententiously "'*The Herald Sentinel Gazette* has turned the matter over to our distinguished legal team and is unable to comment further at this time.'"

"Oh, come on, Tibster – not fair! I deserve better than that."

"I agree you do, and I'll call you first when things are sorted out on my end. Okay?"

"Okay. But you damn well better call me first. And remember, my deadlines are different than those of the broadcast hacks."

"I know, I know. Listen. Let me get out of here before –."

"Yeah, I'm hip. Better move fast though. We're only a few streets away."

"Right. Thanks, Williams. I owe you."

"You owe me big, Hering, and you're paying off tomorrow before deadline."

"I'll do my best."

Mr. Hering hung up and lit out as if he were being pursued by the hounds of hell. Which, come to think of it, he was.

●

"The 'intent to cause bodily harm' suit is a no-go. Hell, we could probably sue them in return for suggesting that you might have such an intent."

"Can we?"

"Calm down, cowboy, you ain't a-suing nobody. That was just Kibble's flashy way to offer us an out-of-court settlement. He can be such a drama queen sometimes."

"But what if I don't want to settle out of court, what if I –"

"Do you have any proof Waldo runs a sweat shop?"

"Well, no, but –."

"It was just a typo, right?

"Well, yes, but –."

"Then we settle out of court. You, or rather your insurance company, pays their legal fees – which in Kibble's case are pretty damn impressive! – you print a retraction and an apology and then we all pretend it never happened."

"But –."

"No 'buts' about it, cowboy. Now hang up so I can call Kibble and get the ball rolling – or rather, get the ball to stop rolling."

"All right."

"Smart boy. Oh, and one small piece of advice?"

"Yeah?"

"Hire a proofreader? They're less expensive than lawyers. Not that I don't appreciate the business, mind you. Just thinking of your cute little bottom line."

"Shut up, Della."

"My pleasure, Hering. You're taking me to lunch next week, by the by. It's your turn."

•

"I always say, 'Never get into a pissing match with someone who buys ink by the barrel.' But damn it, woman, you managed to pull off a real coup today!"

The admiration in Mr. Hegge's voice was unfeigned. He was deeply impressed with Mrs. Kepple's elegant but ballsy solution to the problem. He was also having a terribly difficult time maintaining a professional demeanor and not exploding with laughter.

"Of course you'll settle out of court for attorney's fees, an apology and a full retraction."

"Of course," nodded Mrs. Kepple smugly. Although nothing more than a talented amateur, he understood as well as Mr. Hegge how the game was played.

"Dear me, this has been a veritable bonanza of free media! And all at Hering's expense!" Hegge finally let loose an infectious gale – nay a hurricane – of hilarity that did not subside for several minutes. The only one not laughing was Mr. Waldo, who was understandably a bit of a wet blanket on the subject. Finally his gloomy expression sobered up the rest of the party gathered around Dr. and Mrs. Kepple's gazebo.

"Good Lord, I haven't laughed so hard in years," beamed Mr. Hegge. "You are one smart cookie, Mrs. Kepple. You're lucky to have her on your team, Waldo!"

"And I am lucky to be on Waldo's team," added Mrs. Kepple with a congeniality she actually felt. She patted his knee and slowly Waldo began the long hard climb to regain his usual good-humor.

"Now then," she continued perkily. "Where do we go from here?"

By the end of the strategy meeting, Waldo was feeling much more hopeful. Almost cheerful. He commented on this remarkable change of spirit to his wife later that evening. She harrumphed and went back to her embroidery.

•

Williams broke the story of the out-of-court settlement –
got a pat on his back from his editor for the scoop – and, as Ms.
Della, Mr. Hering's attorney had predicted, everyone officially
pretended the whole thing had never happened.

Once the other media realized that one of their own had
screwed up, they quickly dropped the story out of professional
courtesy. A typo. An unfortunate mistake anyone could make.
Nothing to be gained belaboring the point. The near unani-
mous sentiment was that the public interest was not served by
prolonging poor Mr. Hering's embarrassment any further. The
only holdout in the flood of compassion for the poor belea-
guered newspaperman was Farmer Bob. But that surprised no
one. Least of all Mr. Hering.

Yes, Mr. Hering was the recipient of a great number of
thoughtful and understanding phone calls and emails from his
colleagues in the media. They expressed their heartfelt sorrow
at his unfortunate situation and passed on their solemn best
wishes for the future. Amongst themselves, of course – after
combing their current articles for typographical errors – they
were laughing themselves as silly as Mr. Hegge over the whole
affair, but not a whisper of their hilarity was communicated to
the subject of it. Nevertheless, Mr. Hering knew exactly what
was up and fell into a deep depression.

As for the PAA, PAC, PAL, FPA and various other left-wing organizations and individuals, Mr. Waldo would remain the subject of considerable suspicion.

Somehow Mr. Hering had managed – even in his deep depression – to find enough creativity and spite to suggest between the lines of his retraction and apology that although Mr. Waldo did not technically run a sweat shop, enough questions remained about Mr. Waldo's business practices to warrant a much closer investigation than the quote sweet shop unquote owner had heretofore been subjected to. He constructed it so artfully, that even his attorney couldn't fault it. She did, however, have her doubts about the wisdom of publishing such a non-apologetic apology.

"Does it pass muster legally?" demanded Mr. Hering?

"Yes, legally, but –."

"Then it's printed as written."

It was interesting to note, but not surprising, that even though the left-wing organizations and individuals which picketed Waldo refused to believe anything exculpatory regarding him from Mr. Hering, they were willing to credit as gospel any dark innuendo the newspaperman was able to whip up. "If Hering is willing to suggest he's a bag egg, Waldo really must stink!" was the consensus.

As for Sandy, Uncle Ralph and Farmer Bob – well, they saw the whole thing as part of a vast left-wing media conspiracy to take over the entire world starting with their little village. Waldo was a casualty in that larger battle, and Mr. Hering's cynical attempt to destroy a fine, god-fearing – if a little eccentric – businessman ennobled and even (in some minds) canonized the sweet shop owner. Whether Waldo wanted it or not, whether he actually earned it or not, he had just become The Darling of the Right.

And then there was Mr. Waldorf, the dry cleaner. He could honestly care less about Waldo personally. His quarrel was strictly with Mrs. Waldo, whom he now hated with a hate that passeth all understanding.

Ah, well, if it's not one thing, it's another. That's what Waldo's mother used to say. Waldo struggled to sweep all the unpleasantness out of his mind and concentrate on the good things in life. It took some effort, but for the most part he succeeded.

"Running for office is like playing the guitar," opined Mr. Hegge over lunch. "You can't do it professionally until you develop the proper calluses." Briefly, Waldo wondered if that was a good thing, then asked Mr. Hegge to pass the pepper.

•

Earlier in the previous week, well before the misprint and subsequent riot, Waldo received a phone call from a Trish who cheerfully informed him she worked for a local radio station. He didn't recognize the call letters. She invested a few moments puffing him up, telling him how excited she was he was running against Councilor Millstone and then wondered sweetly if he might available for an interview on Friday morning. For their public affairs show, she added.

Waldo was happy to oblige. Trish breathlessly insisted she was grateful beyond words and very much looked forward to meeting him in person.

By the way, did Waldo ever listen to their public affairs programming? she wanted to know. Waldo was embarrassed to admit that he didn't, so he didn't. Instead, he mumbled something along the lines of, "I think everyone should be interested in public affairs, Trish. Don't you agree? That's why I'm running for village councilor, after all." It wasn't precisely a lie, but it did sidestep the truth and a twinge of guilt fluttered through him. He determined to listen to their programming all week as penance.

"So we'll see you next Thursday at nine a.m.?"

"Yes, absolutely," affirmed Waldo.

And the deed was done. He marked it on his calendar and promptly forgot all about it. Forgot to listen to the programming. Forgot to mention the interview to anyone until Mrs. Kepple called late Wednesday afternoon. She wanted to set up a spur of the moment visit to the local Senior Center for Thursday morning to firm up support after Mr. Hering's retraction and apology.

Mrs. Kepple was not happy with the spin Mr. Hering had managed to slip into the document, but according to the very expensive Mr. Kibble's considered legal opinion, it met the letter of the out-of-court settlement and there was nothing he could do about it. So she determined to put it behind her and move forward. If anyone brought the subject up, she had insisted Waldo laugh (whether he felt like it or not) and ask if Hering had ever written an article about them or a friend of theirs? Or had they or a friend ever written a letter to the editor? The answer was invariably yes – it was a small enough village. Then Waldo was to ask if that article was correct in all its particulars. All the names spelled correctly? All the pictures captioned as they should have been? Had Mr. Hering printed their letter verbatim – that is, without any changes?

She promised him it would work like a charm and it did.

Everyone was forced to admit that, yes, from their own personal experience Mr. Hering had screwed something up somewhere. That admission inspired serious fellow-feeling and it helped Waldo bond with yet another voter.

"So, are you available Thursday morning?"

Waldo stopped reorganizing a display of chocolate animals and checked his calendar. "Oh, I'm sorry, I have another engagement!"

"A campaign-related engagement?"

"Yes, actually, it –."

"You committed to a campaign-related engagement without checking with me first?" Mrs. Kepple was little put out.

"I'm sorry, I suppose I should have – but the woman called me personally and I just said yes. You don't mind, do you?"

Mrs. Kepple did mind, but said otherwise.

"What's the engagement?"

"Some sort of interview."

Mrs. Kepple's hackles rose.

"You made an appointment for an interview without clearing it with us first? You do remember that Mr. Hegge has produced a very carefully worked out media plan? What's the point of having a plan if you don't stick to it?"

Waldo didn't have an answer for that, except to apologize yet again.

"All right, well, nothing to be done about it now. Just don't do it again, Emerson, please?!"

Waldo apologized for the fourth time.

"Yes, yes, all right," bustled Mrs. Kepple. "So who's interviewing you? Surely not Mr. Hering? I thought we took care of him." She laughed grimly. "Is it the high school newspaper?"

"No, it's a radio station."

Mrs. Kepple got a sick feeling in the pit of her stomach.

"A radio station? Which one?"

Waldo told her.

Mrs. Kepple said nothing for a moment or two. Then Waldo heard a sort of strangled rattle at her end of the line.

"Are you all right, Mrs. Kepple?"

No answer.

"Hello...? Mrs. Kepple...?" Waldo wondered if they'd been cut off – but if they had, there'd be a dial tone, wouldn't there?

"Mrs. Kepple, are you there?"

"You – agreed – to talk – to HIM???!!!"

"Who 'him'? I didn't talk to a 'him' – I talked to a Trish. She was very nice. What's the problem?"

"You talked to Trish? Herself? Oh, god in heaven, then it's true." Mrs. Kepple let loose a horrifying wail. "Don't go anywhere, don't talk to anyone, don't pick up the phone – until I call you back," she shrieked and then hung up.

"I don't have caller-id?" Waldo confessed to the dial tone.

How was he supposed to know it was Mrs. Kepple calling him back without caller-id? And what was wrong with being interviewed on the radio? He thought he'd wangled a good deal. Mr. Hegge had told them repeatedly they should "exploit every opportunity to secure free media." Although Waldo had been shaken by his last experience with "free media", Mr. Hegge had assured him it had been an enormously good thing on the whole and Waldo, thanks Mrs. Kepple's enthusiastic support of Mr. Hegge's opinion, had come to accept it.

Now he was in trouble again. "This campaigning thing is so confusing," lamented Waldo . He decided to go back to reorganizing the chocolate animals while he waited for Mrs. Kepple to call him back.

He didn't have long to wait.

"My husband and Mr. Stieffel will be over for an emergency strategy meeting in fifteen minutes. Don't go anywhere!" roared Mrs. Kepple. He wondered how such a small woman was capable of producing such a big sound.

"Yep," sighed Waldo. "I'm in it again."

"But what kind of trouble this time?" he asked a chocolate deer with a dazed expression that closely matched his own.

•

"Damn!" thundered Mrs. Kepple.
"Damn!" amplified Dr. Kepple.

"Damn!" concluded Mr. Stieffel with a thump on the counter that rattled the rafters, shook the walls and upset a chocolate hippopotamus.

Waldo apologized for the umpteenth time today.

"He could call in sick?" shrugged Dr. Kepple half-heartedly.

"Can't call in sick. He's committed," replied Mrs. Kepple.

"Exactly. Backing out now will only make it worse." Waldo wondered how long it might take Mr. Stieffel to wear out the patch of rug he was pacing on so furiously. At this rate it couldn't be long.

"How much worse could it get? Last weekend was bad enough!" muttered the good doctor.

"Worse. Much worse!" wailed the good doctor's wife.

Waldo apologized for the umpteenth time plus one. For the first time in several minutes someone noticed his presence in the room.

"You should be, Emerson Waldo!" snapped Mrs. Kepple. "How could you ever agree to a live, on-air interview?"

"But I thought we wanted free media. Isn't that what Mr. Hegge told us 'to secure at every opportunity?'"

"Farmer Bob's radio show isn't 'free' media. It's anything but."

"Trish didn't say I had to pay to be interviewed?"

"Haven't you a clue, Waldo?" demanded Dr. Kepple.

"Apparently not," snorted Mr. Stieffel.

"We won't be paying in cash, but we'll be paying nonetheless," bellowed Mrs. Kepple. How does she produce that sound, wondered Waldo as he apologized for the umpteenth time plus two.

"I'm sorry, but I just don't understand."

"You think Mr. Hering twists things around six ways from Sunday? Farmer Bob takes the – haven't you ever listened to his radio show, Waldo?"

"Well, actually," stuttered Waldo. "No, but –."

"He's never listened to Farmer Bob. I can't believe it!" Mrs. Kepple threw up her hands in frustration. So did Mr. Stieffel.

"I'm sor –." No, thought Waldo, I'm not going to apologize again. "No, I've never listened to Farmer Bob. Never saw the need."

"He never saw the need!" Dr. Kepple shook his head in rank disbelief.

"My wife has, but she told me he yells a lot and I don't like that sort of thing so I don't listen to him. Is he going to yell at me?"

"You should be so lucky," muttered Dr. Kepple darkly.

"I don't understand?"

"Can you be so naive?" gasped Mrs. Kepple.

"I'm sor –." Here I am apologizing again, thought Waldo. This is exhausting. "Yes, I guess I can!" he answered fiercely. Well, as fiercely as he could muster, which wasn't all that fiercely. Waldo needed to work on his fierceness.

"After the hatchet job Hering's done on you, you're now Farmer Bob's new best friend! It only stands to reason. Oh god, oh god, oh god?!" The undertaker buried his face in his hands. Dr. Kepple made a similar use of his hands. Mrs. Kepple was lost in thought.

Nope, there was no doubt about it. Mr. Stieffel was not happy. And neither were Dr. and Mrs. Kepple. And, for that matter, neither was Waldo. He wasn't used to people being angry with him. Well, he was used to his wife being angry with him. Although not quite as angry with him as she had been recently. For the most part everyone liked Waldo – or at least that had always been his impression, not that most folks ever said anything definite. They smiled a lot around him over the years and Waldo was fairly certain that must have meant something positive.

"Let's make lemonade!" proposed Mrs. Kepple with a perkiness to which she was not entirely committed. Still it passed for almost cheerful, considering.

Her husband and Mr. Stieffel looked up at her in bewilderment.

"Lemonade?" asked Waldo. "I don't think I have the ingredients?"

"Have you gone around the bend, Loretta?" demanded Dr. Kepple, "What does making lemonade have to do with all this?"

"You know the old adage, dear: 'When life hands you lemons, make lemonade!' Well, we all look to have been sucking lemons straight up for the last half hour. What say we try to make lemonade instead?! We came over for a strategy session – let's strategize!"

And so they did.

For the next six and one half hours they prepped Waldo for his face-off with Farmer Bob. They prepped him to within an inch of his sanity. They dissected, inspected and directed every possible scenario they could think of that might arise in the interview.

If Farmer Bob asks A, "For land sakes, Waldo, say B!" If he brings up C, go directly to D. E will lead to F ("if you're lucky") and possibly G, but Waldo shouldn't admit to H, I or J. And heaven forbid if Farmer Bob insists on exploring K or L because there is nothing but M that could be said in reply and that would open up N – an unbelievable can of worms that no one could bring themselves to contemplate, let alone prepare an answer for.

Nevertheless, in time they managed to cover everything from A to Z and back, and they did it over and over again – stopping along the way each time to remind Waldo in increasingly strident tones that if Farmer Bob asks O, Waldo is to mind his Ps and Qs and say R – except if he is asked S, in which case Waldo should reply T, U or even V, but never W – unless Farmer Bob is in favor of X, which he probably won't be, but if he is, then Waldo can say Y, but absolutely not Z under any circumstances.

In short, they stuffed him like a Christmas goose with a "then" for every "if", and enough "on the other hands" to keep an entire flock of policy balls in the air at any one time. They grilled him for hours – stopping only to send out for pizza. At midnight they let him go home.

Once home, Waldo was so worked up by all their efforts, he couldn't fall asleep, and when he did eventually drop off, he was visited by a horrible nightmare. He was being pursued by a flock of angry policy balls until he saw himself light up a cigarette (he didn't smoke?!) and drop the match into a puddle of gasoline while Mrs. Waldo watched in horror from inside the cafe and then he realized he was rehashing an old movie, but the dream was so vivid and realistic he bolted up out of bed wide awake and remained so until his alarm went off at six thirty.

He got up, washed and shaved and dressed, his mind whirling like the contents of a food processor stuck on purée. If Farmer Bob asks X, I'm to say Y – or was it Z? Over and over, around and around, up and down, back and forth, north and south, left and right, right and left and what were pot-bellied pigs anyway and what did they have to do with the price of chicken feed – or was it the price of filberts? And even though he didn't like apple pie he shouldn't admit it and perhaps he shouldn't have had that second cup of coffee because he was too jittery right at the moment even though he was at the same time completely exhausted.

It was in this precarious condition that Waldo was collected by Mr. Stieffel at seven thirty to go to Mom's Fine Eats for breakfast. Waldo was so wound up he couldn't choke down a bite. Nevertheless, Stieffel quizzed him relentlessly until Ron, Mom's irascible head waiter with the ceramic Santa collection, kicked them out "because I got paying customers waitin' to sit down and order, me buckos!"

Still bubbling with unexpressed expletives from his encounter with Ron, Mr. Stieffel drove Waldo to the radio station. He insisted on waiting outside in the car – "I will NOT cross that man's threshold!" – leaving the candidate to stumble in on his own.

Waldo looked at his watch. Nine twenty five.

Perched behind a long desk was a short woman with un-naturally red hair. She asked him if there was anything she could do for him, implying that she hoped there wasn't. Waldo stuttered out his name. She stared at him through her fashion-hideous horn-rimmed glasses and said, "Oh, you."

She punched a button on the telephone in front of her. "He's here." She stood up, disconnected herself from the console and languidly inquired if he wanted coffee. He thought he said no, but here she was handing him a cup and asking him to sit down and "wait for just a mo'."

He dropped his gaze into the unwanted coffee and tried to focus. Instead, his left eyelid began to twitch, his ears began to buzz like a swarm of angry hornets – and without much more warning than that, his brain quietly closed up shop and went on holiday without him.

Next thing he knew, he found himself standing outside the radio station in the rain with an autographed photo of Farmer Bob in what seemed to be a right hand. The hand was con-nected to an arm and the arm appeared to be connected to the rest of him. So he decided it must be his hand. His right hand. He also noticed that it was shaking like the proverbial leaf.

He remembered meeting Trish. He remembered her over-bite and short skirt. He remembered headphones with greasy ear cuffs. And if he tried real hard, he could just recall a speck of egg on some overalls.

But that was it.

Waldo glanced at his tired old watch. It was an hour and ten minutes later than when he'd gone in.

He looked up. Mr. Stieffel was sitting in his car, glaring at him. Waldo tottered over and climbed in.

"After all our work, Waldo – how could you?" was all Mr. Stieffel could bring himself to say. He was shaking as badly as Waldo.

Not another word was exchanged the entire way back to the sweet shop.

Waldo got out and went in alone. He locked the door behind him and collapsed into a dead faint.

●

When Waldo came to, it was an hour and a half later. He was stretched out on the floor of his sweet shop and his phone was ringing like crazy. He picked himself up and answered it.

An extremely irate Mr. Clark of the village poodle fanciers club was on the other end of the line, demanding his contribution to Waldo's campaign be returned.

"I'm sorry, but what seems to be the problem, Mr. Clark?" asked Waldo in a daze. He was groggy with lack of sleep and too much stress and caffeine.

"Don't pretend you don't know why I'm upset," shouted Mr. Clark. "Are you going to give me my money back or not?"

"Well, yes, of course, if that's what you want, but –." but before Waldo could sort out what the problem was, Mr. Clark roared. "That's what I want. My wife will be by to pick it up this afternoon. I'm too damn angry right now to do it myself – I might punch your lights out. Frankly, you'll be lucky if my wife doesn't try to punch them out herself."

Mr. Clark slammed the receiver down.

Waldo presumed something inappropriate had been said in the interview with Farmer Bob. Mr. Stieffel's response suggested that. But what? Waldo couldn't remember a thing about the experience.

Over the course of the next fifteen minutes, Waldo received four more calls demanding contributions back. None of the callers explained why they were angry, just that they were angry. Very angry. Extremely angry. One person could barely speak, she was so angry – although she might just have been suffering from a bad case of asthma. If so, that could mean it was Mrs. Huffnagel, the poor woman. In which case, she didn't want a contribution back. She hadn't made one. She just wanted her usual half pound of lemon squiggles delivered to her front door.

In between each of these increasingly unpleasant calls, Waldo tried to ring up Mrs. Waldo for support. He was sure she was home, but she didn't pick up. It used to be she always picked up on the second ring, but ever since Mr. Hering's interview with her appeared in the paper, she'd been haphazard about when and if she picked up. Waldo couldn't really blame her, but still, it was upsetting and inconvenient when he needed to talk to her – and he needed to talk to her right now very badly. What had been said in the interview? Surely she had listened in? He'd asked her to when he'd left this morning. He remembered her nodding.

Well, if she wasn't available, there was always Dr. and Mrs. Kepple. They must have listened to the interview. After Mr. Stieffel's reaction, Waldo dreaded speaking to them. He would have much preferred hearing the Gory Details from his wife, but if she wasn't going to answer the phone –?

Waldo steeled himself and placed the calls. Mrs. Kepple didn't pick up and Dr. Kepple was "out to lunch" according to his congenitally flustered receptionist.

Waldo decided to get up and go home. He could talk to his wife in person – and take a nap. But first, he wrote a check to Mr. Clark, slipped it into an envelope and taped it to the front door. He figured he could have Mrs. Kepple mail checks to the other folks. After all, as Treasurer, money matters were her first responsibility – and he'd already gotten into big trouble for not letting her do her duty with regard to scheduling. What a mess he'd made of that, thought Waldo. If only he'd had Trish talk to Mrs. Kepple directly, all this hoo-ha might have been avoided. Ah, well, no use milking spilt tears, as his grandfather used to say.

Waldo flipped his "open" sign to "closed", locked the front door and strolled home.

Along the way, Waldo smiled at people and greeted them, as he usually did. Almost all smiled and greeted him in return – although a few glared at him and scurried past, saying nothing as loudly as they could.

Waldo stopped at his front gate and drank in the fragrance of the lilacs. It may be a horrible day, but it certainly wasn't the lilacs' fault.

He took a moment to collect himself before going inside to face his wife.

She'd been acting so unpredictably of late. For that matter so had he. But he – and she – were in the most unpredictable situation they'd ever experienced in their whole lives. This was all the newest of new territory and not at all pleasant or even comfortable. Perhaps he shouldn't have agreed to run for office? And then again –?

Waldo felt more than a little dizzy and his mind was a fog.

The words of Mr. Stieffel pounded in his head: "No serious candidate ever gets himself caught in their crossfire. Farmer Bob and Mr. Hering are murderous with their words." Waldo could attest to that personally now.

He took a deep breath, unlocked the front door and went inside.

"Honey, I'm home!" His words echoed down the hall and up the stairs.

No answer.

"She must have gone out shopping," thought Waldo as he wandered down the hall to the kitchen. He was thirsty and went to the refrigerator for a glass of milk. He was stopped dead in his tracks by a note on the refrigerator door. It was from Mrs. Waldo.

Emerson –

I'm leaving you for good this time. That's right, I won't be coming back. Don't you try to find me. You've changed, Emerson. I just don't know you any more. And more to the point, I don't WANT to know you any more. Not the Emerson Waldo you've shown the world these last few weeks.

I am so hurt and so embarrassed and so – so – in shock. I thought you liked my hats. You always said you liked my hats. How many other things have you lied to me about

*over the years? I just can't bear to think
of it. It's the last straw.*

*Emerson Waldo, are you so hungry for po-
litical power that you are willing to say and
do anything to get elected?*

*I hate you, Emerson Waldo, just as much
as you seem to hate me.*

Good-bye Forever!

Your Former Wife

●

Waldo painfully pried one eye open. The moonlight that
shone through the Venetian blinds was throwing a disturbingly appropriate pattern across the floor. And speaking of
throwing, Waldo discovered a very queasy sensation rushing
its way up from the pit of his stomach. He pried his other eye
open and stumbled as quickly as he could to the bathroom
where, as his nephew had described the experience once, He
Spoke to Ralph on the Big White Telephone. It was a surprisingly long conversation, considering how little he'd eaten. As
for the two bottles of Mrs. Waldo's cooking sherry, well, he
thought he remembered passing them before he passed out.

Mrs. Waldo.

What had he said in the radio interview? Yes, he vaguely
recalled something about his wife's hats, but he thought he'd

complimented them. To be honest, he still couldn't remember anything substantive about the interview. Something about hats – apparently. Some dim something about Korean food, rang a bell. But that was about it. How and where had Mr. Clark's poodles come into the conversation? Or perhaps it hadn't been a remark about poodles that had made the poor fellow so apoplectic?

Waldo washed his mouth out and went back into the living room and sat down in the dark. The moonlight was still making that disturbingly appropriate pattern across the floor, except that now it had moved. It was crawling up the chair in which he normally sat. He jumped up and fled to the other side of the room.

Waldo punched the light button on his watch. It was well after midnight. He knew he should get up and go to bed. But sleeping alone in the bedroom would only remind him of Mrs. Waldo's absence. He opted for the sofa. Besides, he wouldn't have to worry about negotiating the stairs in his current condition.

As he closed his eyes, he told himself as cheerfully as possible, "It'll all be better in the morning!" and tried to believe it with all the pieces he could scrape together of his broken heart.

•

Was the sun always this bright in the morning? It hurt his eyes. And for the second time in less than a week, Waldo discovered he had an exceedingly hairy tongue and a very, very bad headache.

"Ah," he put the two and two together, "The fruit punch at Dr. and Mrs. Kepple's must have been spiked. Well now, that certainly explains some very odd things!" But what those odd things were, he couldn't quite bring himself to remember. He had other things to worry about.

Mrs. Waldo had left him for good. To hell with "for better or worse."

Like an automaton, he read and re-read the note she'd left behind. Finally he got up from the kitchen table and took a shower. He dressed and came back. He sat down again at the table. He stared at his wife's chair for the longest time, empty but for her apron, folded neatly over its back. Then he made himself decide to make himself eat breakfast, although – as the smell of his badly scrambled eggs filled the kitchen – it became clear his stomach thought it a hasty and ill-advised decision.

But it was his decision. His decision. That's what it came down to, after all. It was his decision to eat breakfast. Just as it was his decision to run for village councilor. And his decision to agree to that damned radio interview.

His decision.

"Right then," he said to himself as decisively as he could manage with his head pounding so. "My decision. And if other folks can't deal with it, that's their problem. Leadership is all about making unpleasant decisions. And the more unpleasant the decisions, the more leadership one shows."

He squinted through the Venetian blinds at the big, bright world looming outside. "Goodness, the light is intense this morning!"

He fumbled about his wife's sunglasses drawer. He was always losing or breaking his. She was always having to buy him more. He found a pair that was in reasonably good shape, although a tad out of fashion. He caught himself wondering if they met Mr. Hegge's standards.

"Damn Mr. Hegge's standards!" he growled fiercely. "Yes, sir, this village is going to see some real leadership – starting today!"

He resolved to put Mrs. Waldo's defection out of his mind and move forward. Briskly and soberly. As befitted a credible candidate for public office. He washed his breakfast dishes, made himself a cheese sandwich for lunch (it was the only thing he really knew how to make – other than chocolates) and set off for his sweet shop at a determined clip, despite the ill-tuned timpani cadenza roaring along inside his head.

"Leadership," he muttered, setting his jaw. "It's all about Leadership!"

•

The phone conversation with Mrs. Kepple was not going well.

Waldo paced about the shop like a caged lion. Well, at the moment – if Waldo had taken the moment to compare himself to an animal in a cage – he would very likely have compared himself to a caged lion. But in reality, he was more of a caged gerbil. No, that's unfair. At the moment – although he was rather less than a lion – he was certainly far more than a gerbil.

Whatever the appropriate faunal simile, the conversation with Mrs. Kepple was becoming more and more unpleasant each and every minute. She was obviously in a foul mood regarding the radio interview and getting angrier. She was not happy with Waldo. Not at all happy. She said so.

"I'm not happy with you Waldo. Not at all happy."

"Apparently so," said Waldo as he took the deep, calming breath recommended in the book on stress management he'd picked up at the public library the other day when he began to seriously worry about whether he was in over his head or not.

Brimming with a hope more forlorn than not, he opened lungs and filled them as advised.

It was a breath. It was deep. But it wasn't in the least calming. Perhaps he needed to read that section on breathing all over again.

Nevertheless, he pushed himself to continue the conversation. "So what did I say in the interview?"

"Oh, please. Don't pretend you don't remember." Mrs. Kepple's laugh was full of scorn.

"I don't remember!"

"That isn't funny, Waldo."

"I'm not trying to be funny. I simply don't remember." This was not an easy confession to make. Why was Mrs. Kepple making it so hard? "I was so nervous, I think I must have blanked out."

"Well, I – for one – don't buy it." huffed Mrs. Kepple. "Nervous? Ha! You spoke with such authority. Too bad what you said wasn't what we decided you were going to say."

A sudden flash of red flew up before Waldo's eyes. "Excuse me, Loretta, but I'm the one who's running for office. Me. Not you. Not your husband. Not Mr. Stieffel. Me. Waldo."

"Oh, really?"

"Yes, really."

"Well, the worm has turned!"

Bang! went the receiver at Mrs. Kepple's end of the line.

"She hung up on me!" ranted Waldo to the chocolate animals in the display case in front of him. He stamped about the shop, trembling with anger and frustration. He punched in Mrs. Kepple's number again. To Waldo's surprise, her husband answered.

"Kepple residence."

"Ah. Dr. Kepple."

"How dare you yell at my wife?!"

Now it was Dr. Kepple's turn to bang the receiver down in Waldo's ear. Waldo replied by slamming his receiver down, too.

A moment later, the phone rang. Waldo picked it up and shouted.

"She yelled at me first!"

There was a short, shocked pause on the other end and then a bewildered voice ventured: "Excuse me, I must have the wrong number. I was calling Waldo's Sweet Shop?"

Waldo quickly forced through another of those deep, calming breaths. He failed to achieve calm, but he did manage to conceal most of the edge in his voice.

"I'm sorry. Let me start over. Waldo's Sweet Shop, can I help you?"

"Uh, yes." The woman replied uncertainly. She had a prim little voice, but she sounded pleasant enough if a little wired. "I was looking for Emerson Waldo?"

"Speaking."

"Ah. My name is Millicent Van Houter."

"Yes?"

"I heard you on Farmer Bob's radio show?"

Waldo's spirits sank. Someone else who wanted their money back. He steeled himself for the inevitable shriekings and recriminations.

"Yes?"

Her words tumbled out on a single breath. "I loved what you said about parking meters and I agree whole-heartedly! I put a check for your campaign in the mail this morning. Keep up the good work!"

She hung up before Waldo could ask her what it was he'd said about parking meters.

Waldo sat down and took another very deep breath. This time, he thought the calm might just have begun to kick in.

As it turned out, he was dead wrong.

five

The phone didn't stop ringing for the rest of the morning.

The callers either loved Waldo, or hated Waldo. They wanted to donate to his campaign or they wanted their money back. Unfortunately for his shop, none of them was in the least bit interested in buying sweets.

Waldo tried several times to persuade them to tell him what he'd said that so motivated them, but the callers just laughed – scornfully or not depending on whether they approved or disapproved of what he was presumed to have said. In the end, he gave up. A good three-quarters of them hadn't even heard Farmer Bob's radio show. They were reacting to what someone else had heard (and told them) – or they were reacting to what someone else had heard from someone else (and told them).

Folks were incensed or enraptured about Waldo's views on parking meters, library hours, sewer assessments, tax rebates, public parks, textbooks, developing the village center or NOT developing the village center, kilts, frogs, Pidgin English, red-eyed jacks, women's hemlines, Bosnian resettlement and *coq au vin.*

It seemed he'd been credited with an opinion about anything and everything from potholes to pot-bellied pigs – whether or not the subject was even relevant to someone running for village council. And then there were a whole slew of subjects about which he couldn't possibly have an opinion – for the simple reason he hadn't a clue what the caller was talking about.

With regard to pot-bellied pigs, however, one of the most frustrating exchanges of the morning was with Mrs. Humphries, the President of the local Pot-Bellied Pig Breeders Association. The PBPBA was currently lobbying the village council with great vigor to declare the pot-bellied pig a pet – so that the breeders might be allowed to pursue their calling within the village limits. It seemed that raising livestock was not permitted within the village limits, while breeding pets was.

Mrs. Humphries was furious beyond belief.

"I feel horribly betrayed, Waldo. Horribly!"

Sometime in the course of the past two weeks, she had come to understand that Waldo shared her point of view. And now Mrs. Humphries was white-hot that he'd "one-eightied his position!!!"

The thing was, Waldo couldn't recall speaking to her about pot-bellied pigs – or to anyone else, for that matter. Well, other than to his campaign team. They'd told him not to have an opinion either way and refused to explain what a pot-bellied pig was. "Not enough time! Too complicated!" Waldo wondered if they even knew. Perhaps that's why they didn't tell him? They couldn't. Anyway, if he didn't know what a pot-bellied pig was, how could he possibly be for or against one?

He tried to explain that to Mrs. Humphries, but she hung up on him almost before he began.

Even more curious, Waldo received a phone call shortly thereafter from a Mr. Walsh. Owing to an unfortunate experience as a small child the details of which he seemed unwilling or unable to articulate, but insisted on referring to in every other paragraph (Mr. Walsh, like so many concerned citizens, spoke only in paragraphs) – Mr. Walsh was now violently opposed to the breeding of pot-bellied pigs within the village limits. In fact, he was violently opposed to pot-bellied pigs, period. Somehow, he too had developed the impression in the last few weeks that Waldo shared his point of view and was now just as mad as Mrs. Humphries, because he, like Mrs. Humphries, was convinced that Waldo had now changed his position.

How could Waldo be both for and against something he knew nothing about? Naturally, Waldo was not able to ask Mr. Walsh that very pertinent question. After Mr. Walsh finished the last paragraph of his rant, Mr. Walsh, as so many others had that morning, simply slammed the receiver down.

By lunchtime, Waldo couldn't take it any longer. He slipped on his sunglasses, grabbed his cheese sandwich, locked up his shop, and went for a long walk down by the river.

•

So. Just what the heck had he talked about in that radio interview? Waldo racked his brains.

His wife's hats. Parking meters. Poodles (maybe?). And pot-bellied pigs – assuredly! But what else?

On a grassy knoll overlooking the river, Waldo found the only spot on a weathered wooden park bench that hadn't been defaced by pigeons as yet and sat down. In the stretch of grass to his left there was a handful of shrieking children playing tag. They seemed so happy and carefree. Their joy and innocence made him smile. It had been a long time since he'd felt as happy and carefree as that. Long before he'd ever considered running for office. For some odd reason – but it wasn't that odd, now was it? – the moment, years ago, when he'd asked Mrs. Waldo to be Mrs. Waldo came to mind. He thought about how terribly nervous he'd felt at the time. He feared she wouldn't accept, but in the blessed moment when she'd said yes, he'd nearly jumped with joy.

Now, of course, she'd left him – for good, she'd said. He recalled her last note to him with a stab of pain. Well, at least they didn't have any children to complicate matters. But that thought, somehow, didn't make Waldo feel any better. Quite the opposite, in fact. If only they had had children, perhaps she would have stayed. Long enough for him, at least, to have been able to try to explain, to apologize, to tell her he loved her and needed her more than anything. And even if that hadn't worked, there would still have been a child or two to love him, whether his wife could bring herself to continue to do so or not.

Waldo took out his sandwich and stared at it. It didn't look very appetizing. Why should it? He'd made it himself and he'd never been much good at fixing food, even something a simple as a cheese sandwich. His wife was a good cook, though. "A good plain cook," she used to say with pride. Her grandmother had taught her, the one born in Cornwall, England. "*Je suis une maîtresse de la cuisine anglaise!*" she'd laugh in her schoolgirl French. Waldo used to laugh with her. It all seemed so long ago.

He had tried to admit to Mrs. Kepple (whom he had considered a friend and ally) that he didn't remember any of the details of the radio interview, but she didn't believe him. Not only that, the woman had yelled at him and hung up. Could he expect better from anyone else? No. Hadn't his wife left him rather than talk to him about it?

A pigeon fluttered about in front of the bench and glared at him. Or rather, he glared at Waldo's sandwich. The pigeon's definition of "appetizing" was much broader than Waldo's. The bird made it abundantly clear he wanted the sandwich – and he wanted it now. Waldo tore the bread up into little pieces and scattered them on the grass. As the panhandling pigeon and the rest of his flock devoured Waldo's offering like a congregation of Baptists in search of someone else's salvation, Waldo chewed thoughtfully on the piece of cheese that was left.

What was the point of saying anything? He should just move forward as if nothing at all had happened. Brazen it out. His experience with Mr. Hering, the misprint and the dropped lawsuit was supposed to have taught him that. That's what his campaign committee – and the horrible Mr. Hegge – had told him repeatedly. To be honest, Waldo didn't feel like moving at all, let alone forward – wherever that was in all this mess.

The children were still playing tag. The "it" boy was very small and wasn't as fast as the others. He was having a terrible time tagging someone else. Pretty soon, thought Waldo, he'll be in tears – and then the rest will laugh at him. Children can be so cruel, sometimes.

Politics was such a strange business. Apologies that aren't apologies. Saying you like people you can't stand. Disliking people publicly that you somewhat admire. Being hated for what you say and what you don't say. Being hated for what someone else says you say – even though you didn't actually say it. Saying nothing of any importance whenever possible and for as long as possible. Never admitting you might not understand or know the answer. And above all, always blaming someone else whether they are responsible or not, never accepting any responsibility yourself.

Oh, and yelling. Lots and lots of yelling. Yelling until you go hoarse with all the yelling.

And yet, Waldo reflected, isn't that how everyone behaves every day? It's business as usual, just intensified. Real life, just bigger and in Technicolor™. Real life, but with pictures of you on the television and stories about you in the newspaper. Stories with no more truth or compassion in them than gossip over a fence.

"Oh, dear," muttered Waldo, "I suppose this means I have become cynical."

True to Waldo's prediction, the little "it" boy began to cry. His playmates called him a cry baby and ran away. Even though they called him names, the little boy ran after them anyway, abandoning Waldo to the ill-tempered and rapacious pigeons. The birds glared at him. Every single one of them. Having finished off his initial gift of bread, they wanted more.

"More! More! More!" they squawked at him. "We want more!"

Waldo jumped up and waved his arms wildly. "Go away, you silly birds! Go away!"

And they did. Waldo was left all alone, except for his thoughts.

With the grim tenacity one usually reserves for picking at a fresh scab, Waldo pondered all that had happened to him since he'd uttered those fateful words:

'You know, Mrs. Kepple, it's all a question of good neighborliness. When it comes to politics, why do we seem to forget that? It's cooperation, not conflict, that makes a community.'

He had been hopelessly altruistic.

No, he had been hopelessly stupid.

He'd clearly gotten it all wrong. Community is about conflict, not cooperation. "Good neighborliness" is a myth. Politics – and for that matter, religion – are simply how people rationalize their hatefulness towards each other. What other interpretation was possible, given everything he'd been through in the past few weeks?

"No," said Waldo finally and with determination. "If this is the price, I refuse to pay it. I will not become cynical. I will believe in the goodness of man. I will!" But it was obvious he couldn't do so and remain in politics. Perhaps others could, but he could not. Mr. Carle had been right.

"I will drop out of the race for village councilor," he vowed. "I will go back to my sweet shop, as Mr. Carle has suggested, and I shall fill the world with 'fleeting moments of joy and pleasure.' That is all that matters in the end!"

Waldo looked up, a changed man – or rather, a restored man. In that moment, he'd rediscovered the real Waldo, the one his wife had fallen in love with and missed, now, so terribly. Waldo looked up and saw a very different world thrumming around him, filled with dappled sunlight and quivering with yet to be expressed joy. A gentle breeze rustled the leaves of the birches, the river sparkled and life was good.

Waldo was roused from this blissful reverie by a whimper. He looked about and saw a little girl near the entrance to the park. She was standing all alone and crying. Waldo got up and went over to her to see if he could help.

"Hey there, honeybunch, what's the matter?"

As the owner of a sweet shop, Waldo got to know all the children of the village rather well – but he didn't recognize this little one. She seemed to be about four or five and was clutching a torn fabric dolly. Waldo rummaged about in his pockets and found a couple of toffees. He gave them to her.

The little girl looked at him, and at his sweets, with wide eyes. She continued to whimper, but the sight of the toffees calmed her somewhat. When it comes to sweets, children are so predictable, thought Waldo with a smile. So are adults, for that matter.

"Where's your Mama, dear? Have you lost your Mama?"

The child nodded, still in tears.

"What say we try and find her, eh? You take those toffees and I'll look about, all right?"

The child took the sweets and Waldo scanned the park carefully. The only person he could see was cheerful old Mr. Chong doing what appeared to be his tai-chi exercises. There was no Mama anywhere in sight. This was not good. He came back to the little girl. She was sniffling, but not crying any longer. She had polished off the sweets and was looking for more.

What to do? wondered Waldo, smiling down at her as reassuringly as possible. He patted her golden curls. In a sudden burst of fear and feeling, the little creature hugged his knee. Waldo's heart went out to her. If only he and Mrs. Waldo had had children! Happily, he remembered they were only a few blocks from the police station. He really ought to walk the child over there. Police Chief Gunderson or Elmo, his part-time deputy, would know the proper thing to do.

"Let's go find a policeman. He'll help us find your Mama. All right?"

The child nodded and reluctantly untangled herself from his knee. She took his hand and they set off in the direction of the police station, the little girl dragging the torn fabric dolly behind her.

•

From an exceedingly respectable distance, Mr. Waldorf, the dry cleaner – he who so disliked Mrs. Waldo for what she had said about him in *The Herald Sentinel Gazette* and who, on account of it, had little time for Mr. Waldo and Mr. Waldo's campaign – watched this touching scene with considerable interest.

As might be expected, Mr. Waldorf was thoroughly appalled by what he saw. In fact, he shook with horror. He spluttered with a righteous indignation. As Waldo and the little girl walked away, hand in hand, in search of the police, Mr. Waldorf helpfully grabbed his cell phone and furiously punched in their number.

•

It was Elmo's day off. Police Chief Gunderson was out sick. The chief's chiropractor had given him strict orders to keep his ailing back horizontal with alternating ice packs and heating pads – or he, the chiropractor, "was not going to be held responsible for what might happen."

Thus it was that Deputy Noakes of the city police, who was filling in for the day, took Mr. Waldorf's highly agitated phone call. He'd seen some pretty terrible things over the years, and he took Mr. Waldorf's concerns very seriously. He grabbed his gun and his handcuffs and ran out the door immediately.

Meanwhile, Miss Lorrie Mae MacPherson, stepped out of the park's public convenience. The burrito she had shared with her little girl, Lorrie June, had rather too quickly worked its way through her system. Speaking of Lorrie June, where was she? Not where Lorrie Mae had left her, playing with her dolly. Where was she?! Lorrie Mae ran all over the park, calling out her baby's name. By chance, she looked away from the river and toward the center of the village. She caught a glimpse of her baby's golden curls turning a corner. Holding her baby's hand, and leading her away, was a strange man.

Lorrie Mae shrieked and ran after them.

She was followed, of course, by Mr. Waldorf – but at that exceedingly respectable distance mentioned earlier. Mr. Waldorf didn't really want to get involved. It wouldn't look right. People knew how much he disliked Mrs. Waldo. They might unfairly question his motives. He was curious, however, as to how it things might turn out. Matters didn't take long to come to a very dramatic head.

It all seemed to happen at once and in slow motion.

Lorrie Mae turned the corner and saw her baby crossing the street with the strange man. She screamed at him to let her baby go. At the same moment, Deputy Noakes arrived on the scene. Hearing Lorrie Mae's anguished scream, he instinctively pulled his gun and pointed it at the strange man with the child. As he was from the city, he didn't know who Waldo was, but knowing who the man was wouldn't have stopped him from doing his duty as he saw it. And as he saw it, his duty was clear.

"Unhand that child, mister!" he shouted.

(Well, to be honest he didn't actually say "mister". He used a very different word that also began with an "M." A much harsher word. A street-wise word, befitting the street-wise character Deputy Noakes was proud to affect.)

Waldo, who had turned in surprise to look at Lorrie Mae, owing to her bloodcurdling scream, now turned back to face Deputy Noakes and, more to the point, to face the Deputy's very large and impressive firearm. It was aimed squarely at Waldo's heart.

It should come as no surprise that Waldo promptly fainted dead away.

•

When Waldo came around, he was handcuffed to a parking meter. Deputy Noakes was taking statements and both Lorrie Mae and Lorrie June were crying hysterically in each other's arms. Waldo wasn't quite sure what was going on, but the horrified expressions on the crowd's faces – naturally, a small crowd had gathered – soon gave him an inkling. That and the exceedingly unpleasant remark tossed in his general direction by Mr. White, the baker, in front of whose shop all this was taking place.

"Excuse me! Officer!" cried Waldo.

"Shut up, mister," replied the deputy. (See previous note regarding the term "mister.")

"That kind of language is not appropriate in front of a child," sniffed Miss Hagelboot, a tall, conservatively dressed woman whose statement the deputy was currently transcribing. (She had been crossing the street at the same time as Waldo and the little girl.) Miss Hagelboot directed the deputy's attention to the child with a graceful gesture of her right hand, but it was clear the two Lorries were making so much noise neither could have heard anything but themselves.

"Sorry, ma'am, but perverts make me so sick. I forget myself sometimes when I'm forced to be around them." The deputy gnashed his teeth.

Miss Hagelboot, who was the one and only teller in the village bank, had known Mr. Waldo for years. She was unconvinced that Mr. Waldo was guilty of the horrible thing he was apparently being credited for having done.

"You had better hope, Officer, that Mr. Waldo is guilty of what you suggest he's guilty. Otherwise, your behavior will open both you and the village police department to a very large lawsuit. As one of the taxpayers who will have to pick up the tab for any judgments awarded, I can assure you I am not pleased with how you are handling yourself. I intend on speaking to Chief Gunderson personally."

"Are you one of those civil libertarian types, ma'am?"

Miss Hagelboot ignored his question but noted its tone. She vowed to herself to remark on both to the Chief. "I suggest for the sake of public safety you defuse this situation as quickly as possible."

The deputy wanted to argue with her – actually he wanted to shove a half a grapefruit in her pinched up face (serve her right!) – but he grudgingly realized she might be right. He didn't want to be held responsible for a riot, even over such a thoroughly understandable provocation. The deputy briskly took down the name and address of everyone who was willing to admit seeing anything (four people, including the trouble-some Miss Hagelboot) and shouted at the rest to "Get on with your business! Move along, now! Move along! Do I need to cite you for loitering or interfering with an officer?"

He told Waldo he couldn't possibly listen to anything Waldo was saying until he had him back at the police station. As for the two Lorries, he asked the gaggle of middle-aged fe-males that had gathered to comfort them to bring the mother and child to the station when they'd calmed down a bit. Betty Sue, the hairdresser, spoke for the women and promised to do just that.

The Deputy yanked hard on Waldo's handcuffs and an-grily frogmarched him down the street in front of God and Everybody.

•

Slam! went the door to the village's tiny police station.

The deputy pushed Waldo through the postage stamp sized lobby and into the Chief's private office. It wasn't much bigger.

Waldo started to explain to the deputy what had happened, but the deputy cut him off.

"Here. Sign this, Sir."

The deputy thrust a piece of paper on a clipboard at him. The paper was covered with very, very small print.

"What's this?"

"It gives me permission to search you, Sir."

"I don't understand?"

"It's routine, Sir."

The deputy wielded the word "Sir" like a twenty-five pound truncheon. Waldo winced every time it was swung at him.

"It doesn't look quite right."

"You got something to hide, Sir?"

"No!" said Waldo, "Absolutely not!" and signed the piece of paper in what he thought was good faith, not realizing that "good faith" was a binding legal term no longer applicable according to the finest of fine print in the document now bearing his signature.

Several years ago, the deputy had gotten into a spot of bother over a full-body cavity search and DNA work-up performed after pulling a miscreant over for having a broken parking light. The perp later claimed the deputy had performed those searches illegally and to the Deputy's horror the damned court backed him up and threw the evidence out.

As the result of an administrative hearing six months afterwards, a letter was placed in Deputy Noakes' file. The perp's lawyer had wanted him fired or at least Officially Reprimanded. Instead, a vaguely reproachful letter was temporarily placed in the Deputy's file and the Deputy himself was put on administrative leave for three months with full pay including overtime. When the perp's lawyer objected in vigorous terms that this "punishment" was essentially a paid vacation for the deputy, the lawyer was overruled, found in contempt of court for the use of the vigorous term "patently absurd", fined five hundred dollars and sentenced to a week in the county pokey.

Afterwards, a right-thinking lawyer recommended to the deputy by the Policemen's Guild provided him with the little piece of paper he'd had Waldo sign. It spelled out, in the most exquisitely tortuous legalese, that the perp was giving his full and unqualified permission to be searched, whenever, however and as often as the deputy wished – "in order to affirm his innocence". In fact, very large and very bold letters filling the top half of the document read: SOLEMN AFFIRMATION OF INNOCENCE. These words had been cleverly typeset to distract the perp from the fine print below that allowed the deputy to do everything but.

To protect himself, Deputy Noakes always kept a generous supply on hand and insisted the perps he apprehended sign one. Invariably, they did. The deputy could be very persuasive. Mind you, the legality of this document had never been established in a court of law – but that wasn't the point. The point was to discourage perps from making the deputy's life any more difficult than it already was, and it did.

Mostly.

Having signed the paper, Waldo tried to explain again what had happened, but the deputy told him it was illegal to interrupt him while he was performing the search. Waldo didn't want to make things any worse than they already were and quickly shut up.

To his credit the deputy performed a creditably thorough search. More thorough, in fact, than Waldo's last physical. The deputy found nothing, except Waldo's wallet, keys, coin purse – and three peppermint wrappers Waldo had forgotten to throw away. Deputy Noakes was not pleased. As he disposed of his disposable rubber gloves, the lawman peevishly ordered Waldo to get dressed again – although he retained Waldo's belt, shoelaces, glasses, wristwatch and pants and made him sign for them in triplicate.

"Why are you taking my pants?" inquired a trembling Waldo.

Deputy Noakes glared at him in utter disgust. "Discourages perps like you from escaping, Sir!"

At this point, a breathless Elmo burst in. His sister Alice worked at the bakery and she'd called him about what had happened. He'd run all the way from home.

"Good to see you, Elmo, I'm going to need your help searching the perp's home and place of business."

"Shouldn't we call Police Chief Gunderson first?"

"Not necessary. I have everything under control, Elmo. Let the Chief rest his back."

Actually, Deputy Noakes was less concerned about Chief Gunderson's back than his own. God forbid, Chief Gunderson waltz in and claim credit for such a high profile arrest himself. Before the initial rush of adrenalin had worn off, the deputy had recognized the exciting possibilities for advancement that the publicity surrounding this sort of arrest might afford him – and he wasn't going to share credit with a senior officer. That had happened to him before and he was damned if he was going to let it happen to him again. Elmo, fortunately, was clearly his junior in seniority and intellect and no threat whatsoever.

Nevertheless, the Deputy peered at Elmo suspiciously.

Well, he was probably no threat. It wouldn't hurt to be careful around him.

"You're searching my home?" asked Waldo. "What for?"

"Shaddup, you!" Deputy Noakes waved the piece of paper Waldo'd just signed. "Remember this, Sir?!" Waldo shaddup immediately.

"I really think we ought to call the Chief," insisted Elmo limply.

"Oh, calm down, boy. I'm in charge and the chief's earned his a bit of a rest. Let's stick the perp in the holding cell and drive over to his house and get the search underway."

Elmo wasn't sure this was the right way to go about things, but Deputy Noakes was right about Noakes' being in charge. And about the Chief having earned his bit of a rest. The Chief worked ever so hard. Too hard, thought Elmo sometimes.

"Don't we need a warrant or something?"

"That's what this piece of paper's all about. Whatshisnamehere just gave us his permission."

"Oh, well, in that case –."

Elmo helped Deputy Noakes escort Waldo back to the holding cell and lock him in. He didn't need to ask the deputy why Waldo had no pants. He knew. He'd been given the explanation earlier. Elmo was ever so impressed by how far ahead

Deputy Noakes thought. He seriously doubted he could ever learn to be as good a cop as Deputy Noakes.

"Don't I get a phone call?" wailed Waldo. "People always get a phone call on television!"

Deputy Noakes glared at Waldo. "When we get back will be soon enough for the likes of you. Right now, Sir, you just cool your damn heels."

In the police car on the way to Waldo's home, Elmo asked Deputy Noakes about the other prisoner, the one now sharing the holding cell with Waldo.

"Why do you have Ricky locked up?"

Deputy Noakes shook his head grimly. "Took a knife to school today."

Elmo was aghast. "Not Ricky?"

"Yep. Mrs. Peterson found it in his lunch bag and turned him in to Principal MacNulty."

"A knife?! That doesn't sound like Ricky?" Elmo was having a difficult time matching the crime to the perpetrator. Until today, his only impression of his neighbor's eleven year old son was that of a rather shy young fellow with a stutter and a paper route. When had he turned into a juvenile delinquent?

"You saw the weapon in question right there on the Chief's desk."

Elmo tried to call up the top of the Chief's desk in his mind's eye. It took him a moment. "Oh! But that was a plastic butter knife."

"A weapon is a weapon."

"But it was plastic! Surely –."

"Our job is to enforce the law, Elmo, not question it. School policy explicitly classifies it as a weapon. End of story. You're not soft on juvies, are you?"

"No, no. It's just – oh, never mind. I'm sure the school board must know better than I do about this sort of thing."

"Exactly so. We should have had Zero Tolerance policies in the schools years ago. If we had, we wouldn't be searching this perp's house right now. He'd already be behind bars. Or in the electric chair."

Elmo didn't quite understand the logic in that, but then he was only a part-time deputy and still had much to learn. There was one thing that bothered him, though.

"Um, Deputy Noakes?"

"Yes?"

"Ricky's just a kid. If Waldo really did what you think he did, why did you lock them up together? And both without their pants. I mean isn't that kind of inappropri –."

The deputy gasped in disbelief and horror.

"You just don't get it, do you, boy?'

"Excuse me, sir?"

Deputy Noakes shook his head again, this time even more grimly. "Listen, it's clear Ricky's already on the road to ruin. Probably past salvation. Someone who brings dangerous weapons to school has placed himself outside society's protection. Whatever happens to him from now on, it's on his own head."

"But it was just a plastic butter knife? Maybe he was using it to cut up his sandwich or something?"

Deputy Noakes pulled the car over to the side of the road and addressed Elmo face to face. "I'm going to explain it to you one more time, Elmo. It's not our job to ask why someone may or may not have done something. Our job is simple. Our job to enforce the law. And it's our only job. You know what's the matter with the world these days? Too many people asking why and then trying to explain things away. The law is the law. It's black and white. Ricky went over the line and now he has to pay. It's sad, yes, but it's entirely his own fault and it isn't our problem."

Deputy Noakes squinted out the window at the speeders that kept slamming on their brakes just as they caught sight of the squad car parked along the side of the road.

The deputy shook his head a third time, this time the most grimly of all.

"Society pays us to be tough, so it doesn't have to. We have a mission, Elmo. We're here to save society from itself."

Elmo's heart began to beat faster. He had a mission now. A noble mission even. He'd never really thought of it that way before. Not in those exact words, at any rate. He and Deputy Noakes and Chief Gunderson – they were like knights in shining armor converting the savages. They were saving society from itself!

"Gosh!"

"Now, let's go shake down that perv's domicile!"

"Sir, yes, SIR!"

•

Police Chief Gunderson arrived at the police station to discover it shut up tighter than his sister-in-law's fill-in-the-blank. That, and the squad car was not in its appointed parking slot. Sporting a scowl the size of Cincinnati, inclusive of suburbs, the Chief unlocked the front door and shoved himself inside.

Deputy Noakes was nowhere to be seen.

Not only was the Chief in excruciating back pain, the blistering phone call he'd received from his sister-in-law, Miss Hagelboot, the bank teller, had done nothing positive with regard to his stress ulcer.

The Chief lumbered his lumbar back to the holding cell. There he was surprised to discover a pantless Waldo and pantless Ricky seated on the floor cheerfully discussing the long and glorious history of tiddlywinks.

"Chief!" Waldo jumped up. "How's your back?"

"Not good. Thanks for asking." The Chief stared at his two highly unlikely prisoners.

"Now then, what are you two doing in my holding cell and why aren't you wearing any pants?"

Ricky became very embarrassed and dropped his gaze to the floor just in front of his feet.

Waldo volunteered. "Deputy Noakes took them away from us. He said it would discourage us from escaping."

"Ah. Deputy Noakes." The Chief squinted hard. "And why are you two in my holding cell? Ricky?"

Again, it fell to Waldo to volunteer the answer. "It seems my young friend here was arrested for having a plastic butter knife in his lunch bag."

"What?"

"His mother packed a plastic butter knife in his lunch bag so he could cut up his chicken."

"Oh, Good Lord! MacNulty is on one of his Zero Tolerance jags again, eh?"

"It would seem so, yes."

"Damnation!" With a curious expression that was very hard to read, the Chief studied Waldo. "And you?"

"I'd just as soon not discuss it – right at the moment." Waldo nodded uncomfortably in little Ricky's direction.

The Chief glanced at the boy. "Right..." He unlocked the cell door and addressed the twelve year old.

"Follow me, young man."

"Yes, sir."

"Waldo, would you mind waiting here until I sort Ricky out?"

Waldo forced a smile. "First things first, I always say."

"Thank you."

The Chief returned their pants to them and then pointedly left the cell door open as he shepherded Ricky into his office. Waldo sank down on the bench in the cell and felt only marginally guilty for listening in to the phone call the Chief made to Principal MacNulty. By the end of it, the Chief had made it abundantly clear to the Principal that he considered the affair a complete waste of police time and if the Principal ever dared call him with this sort of nonsense again, he'd lock the Principal up. Possibly even throw away the key.

Next the Chief called Ricky's mother at work, patiently explained the situation – she was understandably upset – and asked her to please come by and take the boy home. Then he painfully readjusted himself in his chair and asked Ricky to ask Waldo to step into his office.

Ricky ran down the hall to the holding cell, the soles of his sneakers squeaking on the linoleum all along the way. Presently he returned with Waldo.

"Ah, there you are. Ricky, your mother will be here in two shakes of a lamb's tail. Would you be so kind as to sit out in the lobby near the front window and let me know when she arrives?"

"Yes, sir!"

"Thank you, son."

The Chief lowered his voice and asked Waldo to close the door and take a seat.

With the door safely shut, the Chief inquired in a carefully hushed tone what Waldo was doing here. As best he could, and in an even more hushed tone, Waldo explained the curious sequence of events that ended with him in the Chief's holding cell with neither his belt, his shoelaces, his glasses, his watch, nor much of his dignity.

"I see," was the Chief's laconic reaction when he'd finished. The story squared with what his sister-in-law had told him over the phone.

There was a subdued knock at the Chief's door.

"Yes?"

Ricky peeped shyly around its edge.

"Is your mother here already?"

"No, sir. But there are a lot of ladies headed this way. They look real upset." Even as the words left the lad's mouth, the Chief could hear sound of the women bursting through the front door.

Realizing who they might be, Waldo suggested, "I'll go back in the – " he couldn't bring himself to say 'holding cell' – "in the back, shall I?"

"Thank you."

With considerable pain and no little effort, the Chief levered himself into a standing position just in time to greet Betty Sue. She was followed by Lorrie Mae carrying a still whimpering Lorrie June. Old Mrs. Windsor, the banker's mother, and Sylvia Fogelquist brought up the rear.

"I understand we've had a little excitement this afternoon."

"That's an understatement, Arnie," noted Betty Sue quietly.

"Perhaps so, perhaps so. But we've all calmed down now, haven't we?"

"A bit, yes." Betty Sue glanced warily at her companions, none of whom looked the least calmed down.

The Chief smiled disarming at little Lorrie June. "And who have we here? What's your name, sweetie?"

Lorrie June looked up at her mother. Her mother nodded. "Answer the nice man."

"L-L-Lorrie June."

"What a pretty name for such a pretty little girl! Suppose you tell me what happened, eh?"

•

Despite repeated attempts by Lorrie Mae to correct her daughter's excellent recall of events and in what sequence they came, Lorrie June corroborated Waldo's story point for point. This did not please Lorrie Mae, who, now that she'd gotten a hold of herself, realized that a fair accounting of events did not place her in the best of lights. When pointedly asked by the Chief where she was when Waldo discovered her daughter in tears and seemingly abandoned, Lorrie Mae burst into tears herself and hugged Lorrie June, repeatedly wailing, "Oh my baby, oh my poor, poor baby."

Mrs. Windsor angrily muttered something under her breath. The Chief caught the words "browbeating" and "poor mother." Betty Sue, on the other hand, shook her head and glared at sternly at Lorrie Mae. As for Sylvia Fogelquist – she didn't know what to think, so she offered to make everyone a nice cup of tea instead.

"Where do you keep your teapot, Chief?"

"I don't think I have one."

Which admission gave a grateful Sylvia Fogelquist something about which she could have a clear and forceful opinion.

"Honestly! Talk about our tax dollars NOT at work! Do you have a coffee maker?"

"Yes."

"That will have to do. Where is it?"

"Down the hall and to the left."

"Men!" muttered a thankfully scandalized Sylvia as she fled the complicated and unpleasant situation on which she couldn't and didn't want to get a handle.

The Chief ascertained that Lorrie Mae was not a resident of the village. She was merely passing through on her way to the city to look for work and had only stopped in the riverside park "to use the – ahem – facilities."

"I see," noted the Chief. He took a deep breath and cautiously gathered his thoughts. "Well," he said at length, "It all looks to me like a horrible misunderstanding rather than anything sinister – but if you wish, you may swear out a complaint and I'll write it up. I just don't think it'll hold up in court and," the Chief now favored Lorrie Mae with a particularly grim expression, "I expect some very uncomfortable questions will be asked all around. I think justice – and little Lorrie June – might be best served by putting this unfortunate incident behind us and getting on with our lives. What do you think?"

Lorrie Mae thought about it, weighing especially the uncomfortable questions that might be asked of her and decided it was wisest not to pursue the incident any further. She agreed to drop the matter.

"In case there are any further questions," the Chief asked for and received her contact information – what there was of it, being as she and Lorrie June were "in transit." Lorrie Mae was not enthusiastic about giving it to him, but lying about her past and future whereabouts didn't seem to be a wise option – although she did seriously consider it.

As the mother and daughter were leaving, the Chief nodded gravely and in his patented Father-Knows-Best voice advised her to "keep a closer eye on that lovely little girl and Have a Nice Day." The latter suggestion was beyond Lorrie Mae right at the moment, but she vowed to follow through on the first starting right now.

"Take hold of Momma's hand and let's go find our car!"

"Wait a minute," cried Mrs. Windsor. "Let me give you a ride to it. My car is just outside."

Lorrie Mae looked at old Mrs. Windsor suspiciously, but then remembered the muttered remark from earlier, the one involving the words "browbeating" and "poor mother." She accepted with a grateful, though tragic, sigh and out the door the three of them went.

Betty Sue shook her head as she watched them leave. "Poor Waldo. The story'll be all around the village in a half an hour if it hasn't spread already."

"I dare say it's in the 'spread already' category."

"You're probably right, Arnie. Well, I need to get back to the Beauty Shoppe."

"Thanks for lending a hand, Betty Sue."

"Pshaw. Just being a good neighbor."

"Never enough of them around when you need one."

Betty Sue grinned, "Just like policemen. Eh, Arnie?"

With a quiet chuckle Chief Gunderson followed Betty Sue to the door and eased it shut behind her. He was heading back to his office to place a phone call to find out where the hell Deputy Noakes was when he ran into Sylvia Fogelquist. She was carrying a pot of freshly brewed hot coffee and a tray of coffee mugs.

"Coffee, anyone?" Sylvia called to her now absent companions.

"Thank you, Sylvia. Don't mind if I do," replied the Chief as he relieved her of a mug and held it in front of the coffee pot in her other hand.

Sylvia looked about, confused. The only other people in the lobby besides herself were the Chief and Ricky – and Ricky was still too young for a cup of coffee. "Where is everybody?" she wondered as she filled the Chief's mug.

"Gone home or back to work."

Sylvia's eyebrows raised unconsciously. "Oh."

"Thanks for the coffee, though."

"You're welcome, Chief. Milk or sugar?"

"Black is fine."

There was an awkward silence while Sylvia worked out that the Chief thought was time for her to vanish as well.

"Well, I guess I'd better go too."

She insisted, however, on taking the mugs and the pot of coffee back to the little kitchenette before leaving. She stopped at the door to the Chief's office on the way out.

"What's little Ricky doing here?"

"He's waiting for his mother."

"Oh?" Sylvia smiled brightly at the Chief. He returned the smile.

"Thanks for the coffee, Sylvia."

In the next awkward silence, while she and the Chief smiled brightly at each other, Sylvia came to realize that the Chief wasn't going explain Ricky's presence any further, either.

"Ah, yes. Right," she sighed. "See you later, Chief."

"See you later, Sylvia."

"Bye-bye, Ricky!"

"Bye, Mrs. Fogelquist."

The Chief went back into his office and closed the door.

He was just about to sit down and punch in the number of Deputy Noakes' cell phone when the front door to the police station slammed open. It was Ricky's mother, Mrs. Dolack, come to collect her boy and in the process demolish anyone and anything standing in her way after the fashion of her husband's new mulching mower.

It was clear from the high pitched screed with which she gifted the Chief, that Mrs. "D" had worked herself into quite a lather since he'd spoken to her on the phone. It was also clear that Principal McNulty, the village school board, the village police department – and in the end, the village taxpayers – were going to rue the day the Board decided to implement a no-tolerance policy with regard to plastic butter knives. Apparently Mrs. Dolack had already spoken at length with a less expensive, but no less effective colleague of Lawyer Kibble – no doubt recommended to her by the Chief's sister-in-law, Miss Hagelboot, who, besides working as a bank teller and as box office manager for the Little Theatre was the President of the local Society for the Preservation of Our Inalienable Liberty. Yep, thought the Chief, this plastic butter knife nonsense might just be the big civil liberties lawsuit he'd been dreading. Ah, well, he sighed to himself, it was just a matter of time before he got SPOILed, as they referred to it in the police biz.

He turned the boy over to his mother with an official caution, and although he wanted to, he knew he couldn't apologize for the arrest and detention – no matter how silly and ill-advised it was. When someone as irate as Mrs. Dolack threatened lawsuits, it was best not to say anything and just shoo them out the door as quickly as possible. Let the lawyers sort it all out later. That was The Official Policy as laid out to him by the village's genial old lawyer, Mr. King.

It took nearly fifteen minutes, but Mrs. Dolack finally ran out of adjectives. Clutching her son to her side and glaring like a mother tiger beset by a clutch of big game hunters, she marched out the front door and slammed it behind her.

"So much for my nice, restful day off," grumbled the Chief as he waddled painfully back to his desk to make another attempt to get a hold of Deputy Noakes.

•

Waldo had listened in to Mrs. Dolack's tirade. How could he not, given her remarkable skill in projecting the voice? (Mrs. Dolack was one of the founders of the village's Little Theatre.) Not only could she project her views, she could also express them quite cogently. Waldo found little in what she had said with which he could disagree.

Waldo was embarrassed to admit that he had not given much thought to the zero tolerance policy when it had been first promulgated. He hadn't read the two or three articles Mr. Hering deigned to print in *The Herald Sentinel Gazette*. Nor even the three dozen letters to the editor that followed closely thereafter. (Over the years, Waldo had come to avoid the letters to the editor page. The letters were invariably written by the same tiny group of angry and outraged people expressing in angry and outraged terms their anger and outrage regarding the angry and outraged views expressed by certain other angry and outraged letter-writers with whom they could, under no circumstances apparently, ever possibly agree. Reading them made Waldo's head ache. So he didn't. Now that he was a candidate for political office, Waldo supposed he'd have to start reading them again, but hadn't quite gotten around to it yet.)

The thing was, not having any children, Waldo hadn't seen the point in wading through the details. In that regard, he figured he was like most people. If a law or governmental policy doesn't affect someone personally, most folks never pay any attention to it. Now that he was aware of it, of course, he was Thoroughly Scandalized. If only he'd gotten involved earlier and said or done something – perhaps all this nonsense with poor little Ricky could have been avoided? And then again, Waldo cringed, perhaps not. Given recent events surrounding his candidacy, Waldo had come to notice that more than a few people seemed quite determined to cause pain and sorrow just for the sake of the pain and sorrow. Is this in the nature of who and what we have become as human beings? Or worse, what we have always been? Even in here in our sleepy little village, wondered Waldo.

"Gosh, that's cynical," he muttered to himself. "I thought I'd sworn off cynicism?"

Then he noticed the bars hemming him in, smelled their ugly metallic smell, and stared at the bare concrete floor. He shook his head.

"Perhaps I swore off cynicism too soon."

Waldo took a deep breath and determined with all his might to think Very Positive Thoughts right now. The time had come to sort all this nonsense out. That's what it was, non-sense. Anyone in their right mind could see that.

With the exit of Mrs. Dolack and little Ricky, it seemed that everyone had left, he'd best to go and finish his little talk with the Chief. He stood up and marched himself down the hall to the Chief's office.

•

The Chief slammed the receiver down in disgust. He kept getting the Deputy's voicemail. Either Noakes had the damn phone shut off, or he'd forgotten to charge it up.

"Freeze, you effing pervert!"

The Chief looked up to see Waldo's face go ashen and his hands rise to the ceiling. Apparently he'd been just about to stroll into the Chief's office, but had been frozen in his tracks by Deputy Noakes' shout.

"Cover me, Elmo!"

Suddenly Noakes barreled through the doorway, smacked a stunned Waldo upside the head and wrestled him to the ground right in front of the Chief. In a flash the Deputy had Waldo turned over, cuffed and his face shoved hard into the cheap industrial grade carpet the Chief had been obliged to furnish his office with so the department could afford the cell phones that nobody kept charged up properly or answered for that matter.

"Now I've got you on a jail-break charge as well," laughed the Deputy with his well-practiced grim-but-triumphant laugh. "You're going away for a long time, pervert!"

"I think not, Deputy."

Deputy Noakes was surprised to discover that he and Waldo weren't alone in the Chief's office. He was nearly as surprised as Elmo who had just appeared in the doorway with a gun quivering in one hand and a big book quivering in the other.

"Chief!"

The Chief shook his head wearily. "Put the gun down, Elmo, before you shoot someone by accident."

With a deflated "Yes, sir." Elmo directed his attention to reholstering his gun. As usual, the assigned task was tad more complicated for the poor fellow than it would have been for most others.

"Yo, Chief!" cried Deputy Noakes heartily. "How's it hanging?"

"Just fine, Noakes. Would you be so kind as to help the poor man you're sitting on up?

"What? This piece of filth?"

"He is not a 'piece of filth' – he's Emerson Waldo, a well-respected member of this community and a member of the local Rotary."

"He's a piece of filth. A child molester. And I just caught him breaking out of jail."

"No, Deputy, you did not catch him breaking out of jail. I let him out."

"What?"

"Now, *you* let him up."

"But, Chief –."

"Now, Deputy!"

'But –."

"I'm not going to say it again, Noakes."

"You don't understand, Chief," whined the Deputy as he reluctantly complied with the Chief's order. "I caught the pervert kidnapping a little girl!"

"Did you ask Waldo what happened?"

"It was obvious what happened."

"I see. Did you ask the little girl what happened?"

"Of course not. She was crying."

The Chief ground his teeth and produced a sound somewhere between a growl and a sigh. "Do you think you could excuse us for a moment, Deputy?"

Although he was now looking anything but, Deputy Noakes replied, "Sure, Chief."

The Chief unlocked Waldo's cuffs, escorted him to the bathroom and gently suggested it might be a good idea if Waldo washed his face, combed his hair and generally freshened up. Waldo thought that might be a good idea, too.

"I need to have a word with my Deputy. Can you give me a few minutes, Waldo?"

"Of course, Chief. I haven't anything better to do."

The Chief looked at Waldo sharply. Was Waldo being sarcastic or strangely polite? Waldo had certainly earned the right to be sarcastic, but the Chief decided that being strangely polite was far more in keeping with Waldo's character as he understood it.

"It'll be just a moment. I'll come get you when we're finished. All right?"

"Sure, Chief."

"Thanks, Waldo."

"Not at all."

After the Chief left, Waldo looked into the mirror. The rug-burned and much disheveled face staring back at him with wild eyes and a terrified expression was the biggest shock of the day. He hardly recognized himself. His knees started to wobble and he sank slowly to the tiled floor in front of the sink and spontaneously burst into tears.

Upon reflection – and in the reflection – it was clear this had not been a good day. And as Waldo was soon to discover, it hadn't even begun in earnest.

Six

"Arrested, you say?"

"By Deputy Noakes. At gun point."

"At gun point?!"

"Listen, if you don't believe me, ask anyone who was..."

"Yes, yes, I believe you. But who? Spill the beans, Waldorf. Which 'so-called highly respected community leader' is the perv-in-question? Mr. Windsor, the banker? I've always had my doubts about him and his hand-tied bow-ties. Or Mr. Stieffel, the mortician? Putting make-up on dead people. Can't be a healthy mind that's capable of that? Or is it one of the village councilors? Biggles? Bland? Who?"

"Waldo. Mr. Waldo."

It was just like one of those tricks with doves that old Lars Pederson was always inflicting on the boys down at Ric's Olde Time Tavern & Juice Bar on Talent Night – only this trick actually worked. One moment Mr. Waldorf was confiding the juicy results of his morning's observations to Mr. Hering in the comfort of Mr. Hering's air-conditioned office, and the next moment Mr. Waldorf was addressing the thin (but well-

conditioned) air left in Mr. Hering's wake as the newspaperman translocated himself three blocks east and one block south
to the front door of the police station.

After having paced in Mr. Hering's lobby for nearly forty-
five minutes, until the newspaperman got off a vitally important phone-call (as Mr. Waldorf had been primly informed) to
Councilor Millstone's office Mr. Waldorf had expected at least
a thank-you.

●

Chief Gunderson twisted his neck to the left until it
cracked, all the while squinting ominously across his desk at
Deputy Noakes and Officer Elmo.

The Deputy suddenly grabbed the book Elmo was clutching and slammed it down in front of the Chief.

"Look at this, Sir!" insisted the Deputy. "We found it in
his bedroom!"

Arnie Gunderson calmly spread the profusely illustrated
publication out before him and stared at it. He shook his head
in disbelief.

●

"I feel so – so violated!" sobbed Lorrie Mae. She noisily
blew her nose into the borrowed hankie.

Mrs. Flick, the butcher's wife – whose hankie it was – was beside herself with indignation. "It's not right what was done to you."

"Not right," came the mumbled chorus of outraged assent from the other ladies assembled in the juice bar portion of Ric's Olde Time Tavern & Juice Bar.

•

Loretta Kepple was absolutely, tear-your-hair-out-and-break-something furious with Emerson Waldo. Not only was she livid with him for what he'd said in that stupid radio interview – that he'd even agreed to DO the interview in the first place and never deigned to tell her (she MIGHT have been able to stop it – it was possible) – she was even more incandescent because her usual escape from the horrors of the world had been denied her. Normally she'd discreetly zap her stress with a double mocha mint raspberry truffle with hazelnuts. Or two. Or even three if it were a particularly stressful stress. But since it was FROM Waldo that she got those incredibly scrumptious pieces of heaven – they inevitably reminded her OF him and THAT WAS NOT WHAT SHE NEEDED RIGHT AT THIS MOMENT!

So she was frantically trying to make do with some near expiry date sweets from the corner food mart – and they were so nasty and downright vicious (Loretta was cursed with a connoisseur's taste buds with regard to *le chocolat*) she could barely choke them down. And that made her think again of those lovely, silky, double mocha mint raspberry truffles with hazelnuts that she couldn't eat at the moment without calling Emerson Waldo to mind – and there she was thinking of him yet again???!!!

She was not, as they say, "in a good space."

Then the phone rang.

You will not be surprised to learn that what she was told did not improve her temper one little bit.

•

"It's the smoking gun, Chief!" announced Deputy Noakes in undisguised triumph.

A long moment passed.

The Chief quietly closed the book and glanced up. "Elmo, would you be kind enough to see if Mr. Waldo needs anything? Sylvia Fogelquist made a pot of fresh coffee. I dare say it's not a shot of caffeine he needs, but it's all we have to offer."

"Yes, sir – but..." Elmo wasn't quite sure what order he had been expecting – but this clearly wasn't it.

Deputy Noakes' reaction was even more pronounced. He was, as the Liverpudlians are wont to say, right gobsmacked. "You're offering that scumbag the hospitality of the house, Chief?"

The Chief waved Elmo away. "Close the door after yourself, Elmo, and thank you."

"Yes, sir." Elmo shot Deputy Noakes a thoroughly bewildered look, but complied with his orders.

•

"Oh, that horrible man!" thundered Mrs. Windsor, working to rattle Ric's rafters.

"Mr. Waldo?" wondered Mrs. White, the baker's wife, desperately trying to keep up with the narrative.

"No, Arnie Gunderson, you silly creature! For browbeating this poor dear creature." Mrs. Windsor reached out and patted Lorrie Mae's knee sympathetically, inspiring yet another impressive flood of tears.

"Who does Arnie think he is anyway?" wailed Mrs. Flick in noisy sympathy. Now that her own feelings were welling up in her, she found herself regretting having lent Lorrie Mae her hankie. Now she was obliged to wipe away her tears with one of Ric's nasty paper cocktail napkins.

"The Gestapo." announced Mrs. Windsor, eyes narrowing with a brutal finality. "That's who he thinks he is!"

"He had no right to take away my baby," sobbed Lorrie Mae.

"Arnie Gunderson took away your baby?" Mrs. White was clearly losing the struggle to keep abreast of the conversation.

"No, you silly woman, Mr. Waldo," snapped Mrs. Windsor. "It was Mr. Waldo who kidnapped little Lorrie June. Pay attention!"

At a table nearby, little Lorrie June was demolishing with admirable vigor a huge dish of vanilla ice cream with candy sprinkles and hot fudge under the watchful eye of Sylvia Fogelquist. All in all, it had been a pretty good day from Lorrie June's perspective. Oh, yes, there had been a lot of crying and shouting, but that wasn't much different than normal – except this crying and shouting involved a lot of grown-ups she didn't know. Or care about, for that matter. They were awfully nice to her though, giving her toffee like the nice man who tried to help her find her lost mother. And that nice policeman who gave her some chocolates. And the ladies here at the juice bar who'd given her three glasses of juice and several cookies and two bowls of ice cream with candy sprinkles and hot fudge. It was looking as though the crying and shouting wasn't going to stop soon, but what did that matter as long as she kept getting really, really nice treats?

•

After the door clicked shut and the Chief was certain that Elmo had trotted far enough down the hall, he turned to Deputy Noakes, painfully squared his shoulders and inquired with an almost preternatural calmness, "Do you have any idea what kind of mess you've got me into, Deputy?"

•

"A scandal, Farmer Bob – a scandal I tell you!" Mrs. Windsor, the banker's mother, was in tears she was so angry. "That poor woman and her child were subjected to the worst kind of inquisition by Arnie Gunderson! It was just like the Gestapo. At any moment I was expecting him to pull out a billy club and start beating her!"

Mrs. Windsor and a small but determined flock of extremely outraged members of Ladies United for Strictly Traditional Standards (less Sylvia Fogelquist who was heroically, though unsuccessfully, helping Lorrie Mae try to put a sugar-crazed Lorrie June down for a nap) clustered about Farmer Bob clucking at him their extreme outrage regarding Waldo's rape of a child.

"He raped a child?" Farmer Bob was aghast. He'd just had the man on his radio show that very morning. If only he'd known!

"I was there. I saw it."

"You saw him rape a child?" Farmer Bob was having a very hard time wrapping his brain around the idea that Waldo was some sort of psychopathic sex criminal. It seemed so out of character. Still, the Farmer'd not been able to predict the success of the Lambada either, despite how obvious it was after the fact. Some things are just too darn hard to imagine. He presumed this Waldo as Child Rapist Thing must be one of them.

"I saw him about to. Which amounts to the same thing."

The Farmer frowned. "Where were you when you saw Waldo raping the little girl?"

Why hadn't the fellow told him about these urges of his, man-to-man? It would have been tough, sure, but he could have worked with it. Waldo tearfully confessing his weakness on the air, then asking forgiveness from The Lord. His listeners would have eaten it up and demanded more for dinner. The Farmer knew that if you beg for forgiveness from The Lord loudly enough these days, you could get away with almost anything. Hell, if Waldo'd played it right, despite everything against him Farmer Bob was confident he could still have gotten him elected in a landslide. Now things had changed. Dramatically. The Farmer's own credibility was on the line now, and that was serious. Why hadn't the man said anything to him? How dare Waldo be so thoughtless and rude?! With only a little warning, Farmer Bob could have had the biggest ratings blowout ever. But you don't get those kind of numbers even with this kind of story without publicity in place and you don't get publicity in place without a little warning. What a waste.

"I was getting my hair done."

"Excuse me?"

"You asked me where I was when Waldo was raping the poor little dear."

"Ah, yes. Right. So where were you? In Betty Sue's Beauty Shoppe?"

"Where else, for land sakes?"

Farmer Bob lowered his voice and patted her hand sympathetically. "I'm sorry, but have to ask these questions, Mrs.

Windsor. I have a responsibility to my listeners, you know." Farmer Bob took this awesome responsibility very seriously.

Mrs. Windsor wasn't going to let herself be so easily pacified. "It's your responsibility to help protect our children from child molesters," she replied tartly.

Of course, Farmer Bob could see absolutely nothing to disagree with in that statement and he said as much to a murmur of guarded approval from various of the ladies. Nevertheless he forced himself to bravely delve back into the questions, so he could provide additional points of color to tart up the exciting narrative that was beginning to develop deep in the bowels of his reptilian brain.

"So you saw Waldo and the little girl through the window of the shop?"

"Of course not, you silly man. Betty Sue has some very lovely ferns hanging in the window." Farmer Bob remembered that now. His wife Lois Mae had taken some starts from them and had hung them in their dining room window. They were very lovely, as ferns go.

"We had to go outside to see him."

"Ah. So you had to get up out of your chairs and go outside. What prompted you to do that?"

"Waldo was raping that poor little girl!" shouted the poor woman in frustration. Farmer Bob was almost as dense as Marcella White and Arnie Gunderson, thought Mrs. Windsor. Why was he not paying attention?

A troubling thought briefly rose to the surface of Farmer Bob's brain. "How did you know that if you couldn't see through the window?"

"We heard poor Lorrie Mae shouting at Waldo, you silly man!" snapped Mrs. Windsor irritably. Men, huffed Mrs. Windsor to herself with a righteous indignation, how can they be so blind to the obvious?

"Ah…" noted The Farmer in a properly chastened tone of voice.

He realized in that moment that Lorrie Mae must have been shouting very loudly indeed. Every time he'd picked up his wife from Betty Sue's Beauty Shoppe he found the hair dryers absolutely deafening. And yet, perhaps the women got used to the noise and learned how to ignore it. Rise above it as it were. Otherwise the ladies couldn't bandy about in that place the prodigious amount of town gossip they obviously bandied about there.

And speaking of town gossip, "By the time you got out the door, where was Waldo?"

"By that time, fortunately, Deputy Noakes had subdued him and had him handcuffed to a parking meter."

"So by the time you actually saw Waldo he was hand-cuffed to the parking meter." That troubling thought began to force itself back to the surface of the Farmer's consciousness.

"Yes. Although, frankly, the Deputy ought to have shot him dead right then and there. We can't have child molesters just wandering about our streets willy-nilly. It's not Christian."

A terrifyingly united Ladies United for Strictly Traditional Standards glared threateningly at Farmer Bob.

"So. What are you going to do about it?"

The first thing to do, he quickly determined, was to quash that troubling thought that kept rising to the top of his brain. It could only get in the way of what needed done to assuage his demographic.

"I'm going to clean this town up," he announced with a firmness that surprised even him. "With your help, ladies," he added gallantly.

The ladies glowed with a righteous satisfaction.

•

Oscar Wilde observed that women call each other sister only after they've managed to call each other a lot of other things first. And so it was with Loretta Kepple and Dolores Hagelboot. As the long-time respective Presidents of the local Ladies' Progressive Thought Society and of the local Society for the Preservation of Our Inalienable Liberty, they had much in common, politically speaking. However, although they generally agreed on the Destination, that's not to say they always agreed on the Right Way to Get There. In point of fact, they clashed fiercely on a fairly regular basis.

Even so, it was Miss Hagelboot who, with a sisterly affection, had rushed to inform Mrs. Kepple of Waldo's predicament. As usual, she spared no horrifying detail, no matter how seemingly irrelevant it might be, in her recitation of the sequence of events as she had been able to piece them together. Consequently, Mrs. Kepple had not been able to call her husband with the pertinent details until crucial minutes had been irretrievably lost. Or so she told herself later.

The astute Miss Hagelboot could tell that her good friend had been extremely upset even before she began to enlighten her with regard to Waldo's current situation. She presumed it had something to do with the ghastly radio interview inflicted on him by Farmer Bob earlier in the day. Why anyone in his right mind went on that man's show thoroughly mystified her – it was simply begging for disaster. In any case, Loretta Kepple was doubtless well aware that everyone who was anyone had been talking about nothing else since it had aired. In honor of that fact, Miss Hagelboot chose to begin her presentation of the latest catastrophe to befall Mr. Waldo with the gruesomely cheerful observation that as horrible as that interview had been – and it had been horrible – "By the time everyone hears what has JUST happened, that interview will vanish from the public consciousness faster than an drop of cooking sherry on a hot grill!" – a remark that had chilled Loretta Kepple to the bone for more than one reason.

Naturally Mrs. Kepple shared nothing of her feelings regarding Waldo's betrayal (as she saw it) to her good friend Miss Hagelboot as she piled stone after stone of horror on top of Mrs. Kepple's heart. As justifiably furious as Loretta Kepple was with Waldo, she would never admit any sort of a breach had occurred to anyone, least of all to Dolores Hagelboot, damn her. Mrs. Kepple had her pride – although in this instance she attributed her reticence to Loyalty alone.

"Deputy Noakes is a complete and utter ass," snarled Miss Hagelboot. "I tell you Loretta, there's just something not right in the head about men who feel the need to dress up in uniforms and wear guns just so they can boss people about."

Dolores Hagelboot had no need for special costuming and props to boss people about. She had her Moral Center – which was far more intimidating. Not that Mrs. Kepple would dare criticize her on that point. Loretta Kepple had a pretty overwhelming Moral Center all of her own.

"I'm an excellent judge of character, Loretta. No one has ever passed a bad check on me. You don't work as long as I have as a bank teller without learning how to read people like the nastily written little pamphlets they are. Emerson Waldo is innocent. Of that I am absolutely convinced. Not that that matters, of course. If enough people believe he's guilty of that horrendous thing, that's all that will matter in the end."

Which was why, proclaimed Miss Hagelboot, she was calling her dear friend Mrs. Kepple.

"Mobilize your forces, Loretta! You haven't a moment to waste! You take care of the politics and I'll do what I can on the civil liberties side. I've already read Arnie the riot act. Oh, as police go he's less bad than most, but the man had no business handing the Deputy Noakes of the world a gun in our name and I've told him so in no uncertain terms. I can only hope it's thanks to a lack of choice that that particular hire was effected."

Dolores Hagelboot concluded on a (presumably) up-note by reporting to Mrs. Kepple her conversation with old Mr. Chong.

•

"It's evidence, Chief!"

"It's an 'art book,' Deputy."

"Only a pervert could call that filth art."

"Right. Did you happen to notice the book had been published by an art museum?"

"I know all about so-called 'art museums' – they spend our hard-earned tax dollars on Madonnas made out of elephant shit."

"Doubtless the Vatican Museum –"

"The Vatican?"

"– has a whole host of Madonnas in its collection but, call me naïve, I don't really expect they have any made of manure. Of any sort of manure, in fact."

"Did you say the Vatican?"

"As for your tax dollar argument, that probably doesn't appertain either."

"Get a grip, Chief. The Vatican wouldn't publish pornography."

Deputy Noakes blinked in suddon horror.

"At least I don't THINK they would?!"

Chief Gunderson buried his face in his hands.

•

Dr. Kepple had learned over the years that no matter how delicate or dangerous the oral surgery was it was always wiser to temporarily close it up and take his wife's phone call immediately rather than later.

Fortunately for Maggie Guthrie she was only getting a wisdom tooth pulled and the painkiller hadn't quite kicked in yet. UNfortunately for poor Maggie all that ensued from Mrs. Kepple's phone call kept Dr. Kepple from returning for so long that when he DID manage to stumble back in in a bit of a daze, her Novocain was wearing off and the Dr. had to inject yet another dose in order to finish up.

•

While translocating to the police station, Tiberius Hering was set upon by a gaggle of irate females and for once the fury of the general public wasn't directed at him personally. It was a very pleasant surprise for the newspaperman.

"A scandal, Mr. Hering – a scandal I tell you!" old Mrs. Windsor was repeating her "in tears because I'm so angry" performance that had worked so successfully with Farmer Bob. "That poor woman and her child were subjected to the worst kind of inquisition by Arnie Gunderson! It was just like the Gestapo. At any moment I was expecting him to pull out a billy club and start beating her!"

Although Mr. Hering rarely agreed with anything the Ladies United for Strictly Traditional Standards had to say, as he found himself listening to them (yet another pleasant surprise – this time for the ladies) he realized that their prodigious Moral Indignation with regard to Waldo was very much in line with his own. He also realized that by taking their talking points and making them his own, he could bale up absolute acres of hay regarding his ability to respect points of view across the political spectrum. A strong selling point with the radically non-partisan demographic. Perhaps if he spun it deftly and loudly enough he might even snare a few of them to plump up his deflating subscriber base. His bottom line had been dropping precipitously over the last several years despite his best efforts to pander to every popular point of view he could find whether it made any sense or not.

And so the LUST-y ladies had their way with an astoundingly agreeable Mr. Hering, just as they had with Farmer Bob. Their righteous satisfaction glistened like the freshly sharpened guillotine it was.

•

"You weren't there, Chief. You didn't see it go down."

"No, Deputy, I wasn't there. That's very true. I have, however asked a few questions of people who WERE there. Did you?"

"Yes, I did, although it wasn't really necessary. I saw it all myself."

"And what was it you saw?"

"I saw him kidnapping the little girl. It made me sick."

"Indeed. Did you happen to ask the little girl what had occurred?"

"Of course not. Saw no need to put her through that hell. She'd suffered enough. Besides, it was perfectly clear what had gone down."

"Was it now? Thing is, I talked to the little girl myself a few minutes ago."

"You did?"

"Charming little creature who, unfortunately, has been badly frightened by a whole heap of hysterical adults."

"You talked to her yourself?"

"I did."

"I've also talked to Mr. Waldo."

Deputy Noakes snorted disdainfully. "I suppose the sick bastard denied everything."

"What Mr. Waldo told me squared exactly with what poor little Lorrie June had to say."

Deputy Noakes shook his head vehemently. "Chief, you don't understand how these scumbags work. He probably told her he'd kill her mommy if she didn't back him up. I expect you would have gotten a very different story from the poor child's mother."

"No, actually. Absent the spin she was furiously attempting to work into it, what she had to say pretty much squared with what both Mr. Waldo and her daughter had to say."

"What are you saying, sir?" The Deputy was just now beginning to sense that his world had started to tilt.

"I'm saying that it seems to me that what we have here is a terrible misunderstanding exacerbated by some extremely shoddy police work on your part. That's what I'm saying."

Deputy Noakes gaped at the Chief in horror. He couldn't believe what he was hearing.

"Get out of my sight," growled the Chief, "until I figure out what I can do to fix things. If they can be fixed. And at this point, I don't hold out much hope for that."

"But Chief!"

"Hello! You're still standing in my office. Interesting. Me, I'm beginning to count to ten. One... Two..."

•

Two tired men sat in the shade of a walnut tree and shared a well-earned beer.

"When we're done, do we pick 'em up and bury them, or just leave 'em for Jesus and Mother Nature to take care of?"

"I dunno. There isn't really much left of 'em to pick 'em up by."

"Good point, boy. Good point. Reach me another beer. I'm still thirsty."

•

It only took one ring for the phone to be picked up.

"Whitman! It's Arnie Gunderson. We have a little problem."

Whitman King, the village's long-time lawyer, sighed sadly. "I know."

"You know?"

"It's a small town, Arnie. News travels fast. And the worse the news, the faster it travels."

Chief Gunderson nodded. "Ain't that the truth?!"

"Not long after your sister-in-law, the lovely Miss Hagelboot, got off the phone with you, she called me."

"That wasn't pleasant phone call, I'm sure."

"Not particularly, given the subject matter, but your sister-in-law is quite the lady and very intelligent and I have only the greatest respect for her. It was quite a long and detailed conversation. The admirable lady is nothing if not thorough. As an investigator, she leaves no stone unturned."

Whitman's curious tone of voice reminded the Chief that his wife had mentioned recently that the long widowed Whitman King was finally dating again. Now he knew whom, the sly old coot. Well, good on him – as the Aussies say.

"So what do we do?"

"I presume our dear Miss Hagelboot was fairly accurate about what happened."

"Knowing her?" Arnie Gunderson frowned. "Accurate to within a hair's breadth, I expect."

"Of course, you know you can't admit to that in public."

"Nor to my wife in private and both will cause me no end of grief."

"It's nothing to what poor Waldo is about to go through."

"True enough," winced the Chief sympathetically. "So what's the plan?"

"Until calmer heads prevail, it might be best for him to remain in protective custody."

"You're not serious!"

"I am."

"That's not fair."

"Perhaps not. But it is legal and it's in our best interest, if not his. Question of public safety, you know."

"Did you say *our* best interest?"

"It's a serious charge, Arnie. We have to appear to be taking it seriously."

"It would also suggest that we believed this nonsense."

"What public servants believe is irrelevant. What the public itself believes is everything."

"But it's nonsense, Whitman."

"I know – it's the worse kind of nonsense – but that's neither here nor there. By now half the town has heard about it and firmly believes it's true – which makes it true, politically speaking, until it can be disproved at some future date. If ever. I shouldn't have to tell you this, Arnie, but if it serves some useful political purpose, it will never be disproved and we need to position ourselves for that eventuality."

Chief Gunderson ground his teeth. This class of argument never sat well with him. He was a policeman, not a politician. He dealt with facts, not useful fictions.

"Anything else, Whitman?"

"Fire Deputy Noakes?"

The Chief rolled his eyes.

"You know I can't do that."

Whitman King offered up a whimsical chuckle.

"As the village's chief litigator, no one knows that better than I do, but it felt good just saying it."

"I suppose it felt good just hearing it," replied the Chief sourly.

•

Mr. Hegge was bone tired.

Politics was not for amateurs. It was a serious business. Sometimes – and this was one of them – he felt that if he had to field one more call like the one he'd just received from that near hysterical undertaker, he'd just tear down his expensively engraved brass shingle, lock the front door and never come back.

But then he reminded himself that this was only a passing, though all too frequent, frustration. His years of experience taught him that amateurs eliminate themselves very quickly – and these particular amateurs had been billed up front and the check had long ago cleared.

The money had been good, but it wasn't his problem any more, thank god.

•

Arnie Gunderson stumped back to the holding cell with the weight of the world on his shoulders. Sometimes, and this was one of them, he felt like he was the only adult for miles around. At the end of the hall he discovered Elmo lounging in the cell with Waldo rambling on about tiddlywinks over a cup of coffee. It was Elmo, of course, who was doing the rambling. Far too cheerfully, as usual. Poor Waldo was just sitting there with a terrifyingly blank look.

The Chief came up and patted Waldo on the shoulder. "Hey there, Emerson, how're you feeling?"

"I think he's in shock," noted Elmo helpfully.

"I think you may be right."

"I didn't do anything wrong," mumbled Waldo disconsolately. "I was just trying to help!"

Elmo nodded sympathetically. "My mother always says, 'No good deed goes unpunished.'"

If there was one thing you could say for certain about Elmo, thought the Chief, it was that he had a big heart. Only a few minutes ago he was hot on the trail of the vicious child rapist of Deputy Noakes' fevered imagination. Now he was Waldo's best friend, a rock in a sea of troubles. And what's more, it was all genuine. The boy threw himself into whatever he was doing one hundred percent and it was always tempered with a generous fellow-feeling. The Chief wasn't sure the boy was cut out to be a cop, but he was certainly a fine human being.

Waldo stumbled into Chief Gunderson's musings. "I want to go home," he said. "Can I go home?"

"I hear you, Waldo," came the delicate sidestep. "But it's not that simple. Deputy Noakes filed paperwork and once the paperwork is filed, there are – um – procedures that have to be followed."

"What does that mean?"

"It means," the Chief cleared his throat, hating himself for saying what he was about to say, "you'll need to stay here a wee bit longer."

"But I'm innocent. You know I'm innocent. I could never – never, ever do – what they say I did. Never."

"What I know or don't know is beside the point at this point. As I say, my deputy filed paperwork and, well, you how paperwork can be." The Chief paused for a moment, angry for allowing himself to be talked into making this sort of mealy argument, then offered, "Besides you might not want to go home right now."

"Why not?"

"For your own safety, you might consider staying here for the night."

"My own safety?" Waldo blanched. "Why?" Then a vision of the riot over his non-existent "sweat shop" rose up in front of him. What would such people do with this new bit of insanity?

He jumped up anxiously and clutched at the Chief.

"Please, do I at least get a phone call? Prisoners always get a phone call on television."

"Yes, of course you get a phone call, Waldo. Who do you want to call?"

Waldo had been wanting to call his wife, but he didn't know where she was. Or if she'd talk to him ever again. He'd also been thinking about calling Dr. and Mrs. Kepple or even Mr. Stieffel, but they were all angry with him for whatever it was he'd said in that radio interview. Oh, that crazy interview.

It seemed so long ago but it was just this morning. Only a few hours ago. And now –

Oh, dear.

"I don't know who to call." Waldo slumped back down on the steel cot like a bag of damp rags tossed into a dustbin. "In fact, I really don't know what to do, period."

The Chief's heart (which was a big as Elmo's actually) went out to him. He barely recognized the Waldo he'd known for years. And even though he knew it was going to cause him personally no end of grief, the Chief found himself quietly suggesting, "Why don't you call that lawyer fellow who socked it to Tiberius Hering the other day. I'm sure he'll know what to do."

And he did.

•

Two tired men were still sitting in the shade of a walnut tree and sharing a third well-earned beer.

"Wudja think of Waldo's opinion 'bout pot-bellied pigs?"

"Din't quite follow it."

"Me neither. Reach me another beer. Damn, I'm thirsty."

•

Edward Kibble was striding through the police station door and into the Chief's office even as Waldo was fumbling about trying to dial the distinguished Mr. Kibble's office.

"Good Afternoon, Mr. Waldo!"

The impeccably dressed attorney glanced down at the Chief's desk in surprise.

"Oh, what a lovely book, Chief. I love cherubs. You astonish me. I never had you figured for a cherub fancier. You are a man of prodigious depths."

"Oh, yes," replied the Chief dryly. "Sixteenth Century Italian Ecclesiastical Art. Nothing better. I expect you've come to spring Mr. Waldo?"

"You have a psychic streak as well, Chief Gunderson."

"No, just good eyesight. That lump in your pocket is a habeas corpus petition, I expect."

Waldo, still in a bit of a daze, had finally noticed the book on the Chief's desk. "What's that doing here? It's my wife's?"

"Oh, I expect Deputy Noakes has something to do with that. Doesn't he, Chief Gunderson?"

"You have a psychic streak as well, Mr. Kibble."

"No, just long experience with Deputy Noakes. He's made our firm a fortune in billable hours over the years."

Chief Gunderson sighed. It wasn't until he'd already signed the contract with the city that anyone deigned to remark on Deputy Noakes lengthy history with Internal Affairs. If only he'd had the staff for proper background checks. But then if he'd HAD the staff... Oh, it didn't bear thinking about.

"So," Attorney Kibble's smile was as broad as his expensively padded shoulders. "Do we need to bother Judge Rome or can you and I expedite matters ourselves?"

•

The clever Mr. Kibble had parked his BMW in the alley near the back door of the police station in order that Waldo might slip out as quickly and, hopefully, as invisibly as possible.

"How did you know I wanted to talk to you, Mr. Kibble?"

"*'...For a bird of the air shall carry the voice, and that which hath wings shall tell the matter.'* Ecclesiastes, you know."

"Excuse me?"

"A little bird told me."

"I got that, but who was the bird?"

"A Miss Hagelboot called to inform me of your unfortunate situation."

"Miss Hagelboot?" cried Waldo as he was buckling his seat belt. "The bank teller! She was there when Deputy Noakes arrested me."

"She claims you are innocent of any wrong-doing. But then she would, wouldn't she? Being a civil libertarian and all. Libertarians always believe the best about the criminal and the worst about the authorities. And they're inevitably right. At least about the authorities. It's very annoying. To them, of course, but not to me." Mr. Kibble's lovely new poison green BMW took the corner rather faster than it ought to have done. "I do so enjoy taking The Man down a peg or two."

"She believes I'm innocent?"

"So she insists. Chief Gunderson, it appears, shares in that opinion – but he can't admit it, of course."

"Why can't he admit he thinks I'm innocent?"

"His hands are tied. It's a question of liability. Strictly speaking he shouldn't have let you out without a huge court fight. I expect he'll get an earful from old Whitman for having done so. Love to be a fly on THAT wall." Mr. Kibble glanced sideways at his passenger. "So are you?"

"Am I what?"

"Innocent? Not that it matters to me either way, professionally speaking," with a decided man-of-the-world insouciance. "I'm just curious."

"I am completely innocent. I was just trying to help that poor child find her mother. It's all a horrible, horrible mistake."

"Oh," replied Mr. Kibble, disappointed. Representing a real child rapist would have been ever so much more challenging – and, frankly, ever so much more fun!

•

It took a moment for Farmer Bob's eyes to adjust to the gloom, but when they had, there was the man of hour hunched glumly over a root beer float – just as Ric had explained to him over the phone.

"Noakes, my man! Do you have a moment?"

Deputy Noakes replied with a disgruntled shrug.

"Can I buy you a drink, Deputy?"

"What the hell, why not?"

Farmer Bob waved to Ric to replace the Deputy's near empty root beer float with a fresh one and ordered a double for his very own.

"I gather you were quite the hero today! Congratulations on a job well done."

"Glad someone thinks that."

"Excuse me?"

"Nothing."

"What's the problem, Deputy?"

"Can't talk about it. It being police business and all."

"Quite right, quite right."

Farmer Bob ordered some BBQ pork rinds to go with the floats.

"Everyone is talking about you, you know."

"They are?"

This was a surprise to the Deputy, for although everyone in the room (let alone the village) was talking about him, he had such a frightening affect that no one had the courage to actually say anything to him in person.

"Yep. Word gets around pretty fast in this sweet little village. Saving that poor little girl from being attacked right there in the public street. Heroic stuff, Deputy. We're lucky to have you on patrol."

"It's my job. Just my job. Nothing heroic about it. I enforce the law. End of story."

Deputy Noakes squinted at his root beer float and shook his head.

"You know what's the matter with the world these days? Too many damn people asking too many damn questions. Some things should be left just black and white."

With that, Deputy Noakes opened up and unloaded more color on Farmer Bob for his radio commentary than was on offer at Black's Art Portal, the village's "exclusive" art supply store.

•

"YOU LET HIM GO???!!!"

Chief Gunderson had never heard the gentlemanly Whitman King so exercised. "You let him go???!!!" was the gist of what the village's official litigator said, although the original was far more colorful, expletive-wise, than Arnie Gunderson had imagined Whitman capable of.

"He's innocent," insisted the Chief for the umpteenth time.

"That's not for YOU to say, Arnie. That's for a court of law to determine."

"There's nothing for you to take to court. There's no evidence a crime has been committed. It's just trumped up, shoddy police work on Noakes' part. Hysterical hearsay."

"Incompetent, irrelevant and immaterial!"

"Are you saying you actually want to take it to court and lose?"

"Yes! Don't you understand, by even losing in a court of law, we win in the court of public opinion?!"

•

Waiting for Waldo and Mr. Kibble when they arrived back at Mr. Kibble's office was an extremely eager Miss Hagelboot and slightly dazed Mr. Chong.

After introducing herself and her companion to Mr. Kibble, she announced, "I'm so sorry for all this drama, Mr. Waldo. You don't deserve it."

"To what do we owe this surprise visit, Miss Hagelboot?" inquired the attorney.

"Mr. Chong, here..."

"Hello!"

"...spoke to Waldo and the little girl as they were exiting the park."

Mr. Kibble smiled at the three of them with indulgence and charity.

"And this is pertinent how?"

"I remember that," chirped Waldo. "You asked if she was my grand-daughter. I reminded you Mrs. Waldo and I didn't have any children. Then I asked you if you'd seen her mother."

"Exactly," replied Mr. Chong, even more chirpily. "And I told him I'd seen no mother anywhere. I'd been doing my exercises there for an hour or so."

Waldo frowned thoughtfully. "T'ai Chi, isn't it called?"

"Actually, it's Yee Ha Chi," babbled Mr. Chong in the best of cheer, thrilled to have been asked about it. "My own invention. It's a mixture of T'ai Chi and country western line dancing. I'm just wild for country swing. Very invigorating. Think of it as a sort of East/West fusion thing. Like refried soybeans! Ever tried them? Delicious!"

Mr. Kibble's store of indulgence and charity had a limit. Mr. Chong tested it.

"Again, this is pertinent how?"

"When this gets taken to court," announced Miss Hagelboot gleefully, "he can testify in Waldo's defense!"

"Ah." Mr. Kibble shook his head. "There is no court case at the moment, and there won't –."

"But wait! It gets better! Waldo told him they were going to visit Chief Gunderson to see if he could help them find the poor little thing's mother."

"He did! He did!"

"See! That completely exonerates Mr. Waldo."

"Thank you, Miss Hagelboot. I'm sorry but Mr. Chong would be quite useless on the witness stand."

"Why would he be useless? He's perfect. He corroborates exactly Mr. Waldo's motive for taking little Lorrie June from the park."

"I'm sorry, but Mr. Chong wasn't born here. And he has an accent."

Mr. Chong bristled. He didn't appreciate being referred to in the third person while standing there *in* person.

"I was born in Texas and have a Texas accent."

"Exactly. A Chinaman with a Texas accent? It would make no sense whatsoever to the average juror. They'd refuse to believe anything he said."

"That's outrageous!" protested Miss Hagelboot, her hackles as the President of the local Society for the Preservation of Our Inalienable Liberty rising.

"I'm just as outraged as you are," replied the attorney in a tone of voice the suggested quite the opposite. "But it's How Things Work."

"But how do we clear his name if he doesn't –."

"I appreciate your concern Miss Hagelboot, but, trust me, Mr. Waldo really doesn't want to fight this in a court of law. It'll only make matters worse. Let's just see if we can get it shifted –."

"But I want to clear my name," insisted Waldo.

"An understandable goal, to be sure," smiled Mr. Kibble, patting Waldo verbally on the head. "But once you decide to run for public office, your name is no longer your own. And as for clearing it, dear Mr. Waldo, you're a politician now. Your name can never be clear again. Anything anyone wants to be-

lieve about you and say, they can – and more to the point –
they will. Get over it and move on."

"But –."

"You're no longer a private citizen, Mr. Waldo. You're the
most public of public properties."

Waldo peered at his solicitor solicitously.

"Hmmm. Like a park bench with bird droppings on top
and old bubble gum stuck to the bottom?"

"Excuse me?"

"Nothing," muttered Waldo glumly.

"Oh." The lawyer blinked. "I see. You're trying to insert a
little levity. Very droll. That's the spirit, Mr. Waldo!"

Mr. Kibble clapped his hands and rubbed them together
enthusiastically.

"By the way, is my fee this time on your nickel or your
campaign's?"

●

Mr. Hering snapped at his prey as it left Ric's Olde Time
Tavern & Juice Bar.

"Noakes! Deputy Noakes! Do you have a moment?"

"He has no comment," barked Farmer Bob fiercely, suddenly manifesting in the doorway behind the Deputy. Mr.
Hering blinked and dropped his prey in surprise and horror,
but the irresistible momentum of the juiciest of stories shoved
him forward and made him try to snap it up again.

"Can I buy you a drink, Deputy?"

Noakes glared at Mr. Hering.

"I'm on duty. Or at least I was. Might still be. Dunno."

"Don't talk to him, Noakes. He'll twist your words until you can't even recognize them." A process with which Farmer Bob was himself quite adept.

Mr. Hering ignored his arch-nemesis. Not easy with a man of the Farmer's literal as well as figurative bulk.

"What's the problem, Deputy?" Hering struggled to adopt a sympathetic bonhomie but the Farmer's presence was effectively neutralizing it.

"Come on, talk to me, Noakes?" he was forced to beg.

The deputy snorted. "Nothing for me to say to the likes of you, newspaperman."

"Deputy, please –."

Encouraged by the Farmer's presence, Noakes finally began to feel more like himself.

"Move along now or I'll have to cite you for loitering. You want to be cited for loitering? It carries a hefty fine, you know."

"But Deputy –."

"I could also cite you for interfering with police business. That's a felony. You angling for a felony rap, fishwrapman?"

Farmer Bob smirked at his rival as he and the Deputy strolled away. Mr. Hering glowered as he was obliged to tramp off in the other direction.

•

"You have to drop out of the race. Tell him he has to drop out of the race. You have to apologize for everything and then drop out of the race. Oh, but not admit anything. Dear God, don't admit anything! Never admit anything! Never, never, never!"

"But I'm innocent."

"First, he has to 'suspend his campaign' – only then does he get to drop out of the race. This sort of thing requires a very delicate timing. It can't be done precipitously."

"I'm innocent."

"Perhaps he could throw himself on the mercy of Jesus? Do the whole begging for forgiveness from The Lord thing. It worked for Councilor Biggles when he got caught shoplifting that frilly underwear."

"But I'm innocent. He wasn't."

"Are you actually suggesting Waldo continue his campaign?"

"Of course not, it's just the mercy of Jesus thing will help re-habilitate our – I mean *his* reputation faster."

"I'm innocent."

"Pastor Pat would be thrilled for the photo op."

"Um, perhaps not, considering his problem last year?"

"Pshaw. No one remembers that anymore. Old news."

"Not so old if anyone makes the connection."

"Did I mention I'm innocent?"

"Delores Hagelboot reminded me that the best that can be said about a scandal is that if it's bad enough no one will remember the previous one. Perhaps we can find a worse scandal to drown this one out?"

"Worked for Pastor Pat."

"And Councilor Biggles!"

"Interesting strategy. Any ideas as to where we could find that big of scandal?"

"No. I'm just saying that Delores –."

"This is all beside the point. Waldo has to drop out of the race immediately and we have to put out a press release apologizing for everything. But we mustn't admit to anything while apologizing. Never admit to anything. Never, never, never. That's what Mr. Hegge said."

"But I'm innocent."

"Stop interrupting, Waldo!"

"I'm innocent."

"What is he saying? Someone tell me what he is saying?"

"He's saying he's innocent."

"Oh, please, that's so totally irrelevant. He was arrested. That's all that matters. He can't run a campaign from behind bars."

"Strictly speaking, he's not behind bars. Chief Gunderson let him out."

"But Arnie shouldn't have let him out, don't you understand?"

"Councilor Flothrew ran a campaign while under indictment for tax evasion. And won re-election. And she was guilty as sin."

"Of tax evasion. No one cares about a tax evasion. Besides, she paid the fines. That's all that matters."

"And yet she ran on the Fiscal Responsibility ticket?"

"And Biggles the shoplifter ran on the Law & Order ticket. Are you trying to make some sort of point? Because it's eluding me. We're talking about you here, Waldo."

"And I'm tell you I'm innocent."

"Irrelevant. Totally irrelevant. Somebody please tell him how totally irrelevant that is!"

And so it went. On and on. Around and around. Up and down. Left and right. Eventually, Waldo simply got up and left.

Not surprisingly, they didn't even notice.

seven

Pastor Pat's Friendly Bible Study had some rough going that evening. Oh, it started as it usually did, innocently enough with a prayer or two, but then a veritable tsunami of Current Events had overwhelmed those assembled and washed them all out to some very deep waters indeed. It was all about Waldo, of course. What had happened to Waldo had been violently echoing back and forth amongst the congregation all afternoon – like a wrench dropped into an empty steel drum – and when Bible Study came around, the subject simply could not be avoided. Not that anyone actually tried. And although the Bible Study was always friendly, this particular Conversation was decidedly not.

It was quickly established that Waldo's interview that morning with Farmer Bob had been viewed favorably by most folks – at least the bits that made sense. The most widely held theory was that Waldo must have had a drink or three beforehand. Some of answers he'd come up with had been just a little too bizarre for any other explanation.

But when Waldo had been caught raping that little girl, right there in public outside in the middle of Main Street in front of Betty Sue's Beauty Shoppe – well, it kind of sucked all the oxygen out of any other possible conversations for the rest of the day.

When Uncle Ralph and his nephew Sandy wandered into Pastor Pat's Friendly Bible Study that evening they were floored by what was being discussed. They'd been out drinking beer and shooting gray squirrels all day using their expensive new gun sights with the Bible quotes on them, helping rid a friend's walnut orchard of an infestation of the nasty little varmints and hadn't heard a thing. Well, they had heard the interview. Uncle Ralph and Sandy never missed Farmer Bob's show, but right after that, they'd climbed into Uncle Ralph's pickup truck and driven to the orchard.

Ralph was particularly upset with the news about Waldo.

Not that a manly man like Ralph could ever say such a thing out loud let alone to himself, but Ralph felt *violated* by the news. Betrayed. And not in a small way.

He was Christian. Proud to be a Christian. And as a Christian he struggled hard to forgive other people their sins. But this particular sin really rankled him to the core of his being.

Of course Waldo had those kinds of urges about little girls. Ralph had them, too. Everyone did. It was perfectly natural, given the sinful nature of man. The thing was not to act on those urges. And certainly not to get caught acting on them right there in public outside in the middle of Main Street in front of Betty Sue's Beauty Shoppe. It wasn't Christian.

Uncle Ralph had forgiven a lot over the course of his life. Too much, probably. Or so he thought most of the time.

He'd forgiven his wife for divorcing him.

He'd forgiven his last boss for firing him.

He'd forgiven Councilor Flothrew for cheating on her taxes and lying about it. And Councilor Biggles for shoplifting lady's underthings. He had even gone as far as to work for both their successful re-elections.

He'd even forgiven Pastor Pat for that picture featuring, for Ralph at least, a very uninteresting portion of Pastor Pat's anatomy that had made it somehow onto the Internet. Ralph actually hadn't seen the picture because he didn't have the Internet, but he'd heard about it from friends in the city who had. It apparently left very little to the imagination. And yet Ralph had found it within himself to forgive the Pastor. After all, the Pastor's wife had forgiven her husband. If she could forgive, far be it from Ralph not to.

He was, however, still working on forgiving the choir boy who'd posted the picture in the first place. When he was found out, the boy had claimed that Pastor Pat had been his gay lover – which was simply ridiculous. If Pastor Pat had been a homo, his wife would never have taken him back. Even so, Uncle Ralph had mostly forgiven the boy. After all he was a kid. Kids do dumb things.

But Waldo?

Waldo was an entirely different kettle of fish.

Something had to be done about Waldo and Uncle Ralph knew exactly what that should be. He'd had a Vision while taking care of business in the men's room.

After Bible Study – and in a sort of prophetic daze – Uncle Ralph drove Sandy down to Waldo's shop and treated the boy to a pinch of snoose and a good, old-fashioned come-to-Jesus exegesis along the way.

•

Waldo arrived very late – and very alone – for Candidates' Night at the high school library.

He'd left the Kepples arguing in their living room with Mr. Stieffel about the right way to suspend or close down his campaign. The funny thing was, the more they had whinged on about how important it was for him to quit, the less motivated he became to quit. That he had arrived on their doorstep resolutely wanting to quit now appeared quite beside the point.

"Well," he had found himself saying to himself, "they may be the type of people to give up when the going gets tough, but I'm not."

So far he'd managed to sacrifice his wife and his good name to this stupid campaign, and if those sacrifices had been made, he was bound and determined that they were not going to be made in vain. The hell with going back to his sweet shop and filling the world with Mr. Carle's "fleeting moments of joy and pleasure" – Waldo decided this village didn't deserve that. More to the point, it didn't need that. What it needed was Change – and that was something he could bring them. He wasn't Millstone or Biggles or Bland or any of the other predictable "mealy mouthed panderers" as Mrs. Kepple had ever so correctly identified them. He was Different. He was The Future. And so he determined to "screw his courage to the sticking-place, and not fail" and get himself properly elected. No matter what. Full steam ahead. Damn the torpedoes and any icebergs lurking out there, this little village was going to get a dose of Real Reform. And he was the man to make it happen, dammit.

So there he stood, all by himself, at the door to the Candidates' Night. No wife, no campaign staff, no attorney, no vacuum-packed generic speech that meant anything to anybody. He was just Waldo. Nothing more, nothing less. The Real Thing. He took a deep breath and manfully opened the door and crossed the threshold.

Given the unfortunate events of the unfortunate day, from the unfortunate interview to the unfortunate attempt to help an unfortunate little girl, he was not in the least surprised to find a huge crowd on the other side of that door. Far larger than any other crowd over the entire course of the campaign. (Except for that crowd of crazy people from the city who protested his non-existent "sweat shop." That had been the largest crowd to date. But never mind.)

And yes, although his late appearance was greeted by loud catcalls featuring a wide variety of not very imaginative expletives, he was also surprised and a little encouraged to discover pools of support scattered about the room. In fact, if he squinted just right and made allowances for the villagers who he knew were always opposed to everything and every candidate, he could almost convince himself that the assembly looked to be pretty evenly divided between the jeers and cheers. It was possible.

An atypically short-tempered Whitman King, distinguished emcee for the evening, managed to calm the crowd down enough so that Councilor Biggles could finish his prepared remarks. Biggles and his collection of frilly underwear were running for re-election for the fifth time unopposed.

Waldo took his seat next to an unusually reserved Councilor Millstone. At all the events during the campaign so far at which they'd both appeared, the Councilor had been effusively friendly. Waldo could see that the extremely unforeseen events of the afternoon had left the Councilor confused as to the correct campaign protocol to follow. Be too friendly and risk offending those undecideds who currently believe Waldo guilty or be too unfriendly and risk offending those undecideds who currently believe him innocent. As the Councilor well knew, what an undecided voter believes about a candidate shifts dramatically over the course of a campaign. Never offend an undecided voter this late in the campaign, even if in the process you offend a supporter. Supporters will put up with ever so much more than undecideds – who are, in their affections, as fickle as the spring weather.

Councilor Millstone spoke first, neatly filling his allotted three minutes to the millisecond. As usual, Waldo was never quite sure what it was the Councilor actually said – but after having consulted with the horrifying Mr. Hegge, he now understood why Millstone's views were so, as it were, firmly nebulous.

Mostly though, Waldo spent these last few moments before taking the podium himself, to step back and ponder the larger view of all that had happened today and over the entire campaign. He still had no idea what it was he'd said during that damned radio interview, but that was not going to be his fate tonight. Tonight he was calm, in control and his thoughts were in perfect order. Whether the public wanted to hear what he had to say or not, he was determined that they were going to listen to it. No more sidestepping or dissembling, tonight he was going to speak from his heart and, like it or lump it, to-night they were going to hear from the real Waldo – and in spades.

•

Farmer Bob and Mr. Hering had been eyeing each other surreptitiously all evening, keeping track of with whom the other was speaking and what the other might be speaking about.

The newspaperman carefully observed Waldo ascend to the podium. Mr. Hering and his camera, the one with extra strong flashbulb, were lurking as usual to the side of the crowd. It gave him the opportunity to snap unexpected – and inevitably unflattering – images of people in the audience. This was always the most popular aspect of his campaign coverage. He'd learned years ago as a cub reporter that folks love to see their neighbors looking stupid, funny or bored in crowd shots. Of course folks weren't happy about seeing themselves like that, but Hering had a gift for not repeating a face too often – unless it was to make some sly editorial point.

Farmer Bob also carefully observed Waldo ascend to the podium. He and his lovely wife Lois Mae had ensconced themselves in the fourth row back amongst a clutch of loyal fans. Lois Mae had been looking on tidily all evening as her husband vigorously expressed their mutual opinion – she always agreed with her husband about everything – in public, that is. At home it was another matter entirely. They had beautifully placed themselves for one of Mr. Hering's notorious "candid" photos. Not that Hering would deign to photograph either of them – unless forced to – that was not how the game was played.

As Waldo opened his mouth to speak, in a carefully orchestrated fit of Moral Indignation – a particular specialty of his – Farmer Bob suddenly leapt up and threw a real, honest-to-God cowpat in Waldo's general direction. It missed Waldo, of course – the Farmer had poor hand/eye coordination – but it splattered near enough to cause some minor aesthetical damage to the podium. (Lois Mae had heroically smuggled the cowpat into the hall enclosed in an extra large Ziploc™ freezer bag which she had hidden in her purse under three of her Great Grandma Min's scented and tatted hankies.)

And with that, the "all hell" that had been building over the course of the day – that had been building over the course of the entire campaign – finally broke loose.

The assembled multitude erupted as one into a tremendous, overwhelming, cacophonous eructation of shrieks, shouts, squawks and general caterwauling – full-blooded horror and white-hot fury, loathsome hilarity and heartrending surprise all wrapped up inextricably into a single, devastating explosion of sound. It rolled over Waldo as ruthless, relentless and remorseless as a pyroclastic flow, silencing him. Even with the state-of-the-art sound system provided, he knew he couldn't be heard and there was no point in trying. He knew now, finally, that this damned campaign was over, his absurd dream fully evaporated. He knew now, finally, that no one was in the least interested in hearing what he had to say. He knew now, finally, that they never had been.

So, quietly, he gathered his few notes, straightened his jacket, walked off the stage, out the door and into the night.

Naturally, no one noticed.

Instead, the mob in bizarre and vicious thrall with its own bad self, hungrily cast aside its every restraint and in ecstatic glee consecrated the dank, primordial madness that belched upward from the darkest, nastiest, most mephitic, demon-infested chasm of its collective soul. Punches were thrown – as were a wide assortment of chairs and hats and purses and the occasional half-eaten burrito. Clothing was rent and stockings run. Hair was ripped out and teeth were shoved in. Gobbets of blood and spit flew back and forth with a wild and, dare one say, frolicsome abandon. It was worse than a heavy metal double-bill cancelled at the last minute.

It was the very essence of modern political discourse.

•

Once outside, Waldo looked up and stared at the moon staring back at him. He felt the sudden urge to tear off his clothes and bay at it. Instead, he decided it wiser to walk home the long way and just think.

•

Still in the library, while snapping pictures of the mayhem, Mr. Hering was fuming about the cowpat. He knew that Farmer Bob knew that he would have to take a picture of the cowpat, since it started the whole shebang. Mr. Hering knew that Farmer Bob knew that Mr. Hering knew that Mr. Hering's subscribers would demand a picture of Farmer Bob's cowpat. And so, even though Mr. Hering hated giving Farmer Bob even a column inch, he knew he had no choice about reporting the fact of the cowpat. Farmer Bob, once again, had managed to manipulate Mr. Hering into doing something Mr. Hering really didn't want to do.

Mr. Hering would, of course, put the whole incident in the worst possible light – not at all difficult – but that wouldn't bother Farmer Bob in the least. As far as Farmer Bob would be concerned it would just show Mr. Hering up for the vicious little scumbag Farmer Bob's partisans said he was. And Farmer Bob could, justifiably, be Righteously Indignant for at least two weeks over his treatment. More if Mr. Hering rose to the occasion and did the cowpat justice – as of course he would, being Mr. Hering.

And yet, Mr. Hering told himeslf, the more Righteously Indignant Farmer Bob got on air over Mr. Hering's handling of the cowpat, the more newspapers Mr. Hering would sell. As incandescently outraged as he was at Farmer Bob – and vice versa – neither of them ever lost sight of the fact that for all the venom spewed, it was essentially a win-win proposition. Not for Waldo, of course. But that was Waldo's problem not theirs.

Where was Waldo? Mr. Hering wondered suddenly. He wondered this at the very same time as Farmer Bob. They both knew the thought had arrived simultaneously deep in their respective reptilian brains because in the midst of the madness they had suddenly found themselves staring at each other with the same surprised expression. Then, as one, they had turned to note a platform empty of Waldo but full of Biggles and Millstone, all crouched down behind the podium clutching a bewildered Whitman King. As one they turned back to glare at each other yet again.

Where had Waldo gone? How dare he start such a riot and then waltz off as if he were somehow innocent of it. The look in both Mr. Hering's and Farmer Bob's eye suggested to the other that for the first time ever they were in total agreement about something – and not only that, they were both thrilled to be in total agreement. It was an Historic Moment, to be sure. Perhaps never to be repeated.

•

"Matthew 13:41," announced Uncle Ralph as they rolled down the empty alley behind all the Main Street storefronts.

Sandy stopped sucking on his snoose and turned to his uncle. "Excuse me, Uncle Ralph?"

"It's our mission, boy."

"Our mission?"

"'*The Son of man* – '" intoned Uncle Ralph.

"Jesus?"

"Jesus. Yes, exactly. Jesus."

"We're on a mission for Jesus?"

"Sort of. Now quiet down and lemme quote the Scripture properly. '*The Son of man shall send forth his angels*' –." That's us. Well, sort of. We're acting on their behalf at any rate.

"We're working on behalf of angels who are working on behalf of Jesus?"

Uncle Ralph glanced at his confused but hopeful nephew and set the parking brake.

"These days the angels are just too damn busy to deal with EVERY little problem. That's why we need to step in and help them out every now and then."

Sandy nodded agreeably as they climbed out of the pickup truck. As usual, Uncle Ralph made perfect sense.

"'*… and they shall gather out of his kingdom all things that offend, and them which do iniquity.*'" That's Waldo and his sweet shop here."

Ralph waved at the rear of Waldo's shop looming up before them in the dark. He took a crowbar out of the back of the truck and forced open the back door.

"Chocolate, you know, is a right wicked thing. Anyway, that's what my ex – your Aunt Rhoda – used to say. 'Get thee behind me, Satan, " she'd say and slap her butt every time she ate some. I always thought it was a joke, but I see now that it wasn't."

Uncle Ralph continued his exegesis with rising excitement and began unpacking the big cans he kept in the back of the truck just in case there was a national emergency. This Waldo thing counted as an emergency. Perhaps not a national one, but certainly a moral emergency. And a really big moral emergency at that.

" ' "'... *and they shall gather out of his kingdom all things that offend, and them which do iniquity. And shall cast them into a furnace of fire,'*"

"A furnace of FIRE?!"

Sandy finally registered the gas cans in his Uncle's grip and stared at them in shock.

"Yep. And that's exactly what we're about to take care of right now. Cast them into a furnace of fire." He handed Sandy two of the cans and took two himself.

"We're going to burn down Mr. Waldo's sweet shop?" This was not exactly the heavenly mission he'd imagined.

"Cast it into a furnace of fire, praise the Lord."

Sandy frowned nervously as they carried the gas cans into Waldo's backroom. "What about Mr. Waldo? Are we going to cast him into this furnace too? Are we going to burn him up too?"

Uncle Ralph hadn't actually thought that far quite yet. But the answer came easily enough. When you're on a mission for God, Ralph always found, answers were right there on the tip of your tongue when needed.

"Um – that's the bit we leave to the angels. Yeah. After all it's THEIR job not ours. We're just helping them out a bit. Right?"

"Right," agreed Sandy uncertainly.

"Oh, and the Scripture goes on, you know. '... *there shall be wailing and gnashing of teeth.*' That's the bit that refers to his friend Dr. Kepple, the dentist. See. God thinks of everything. Even puts a reference into the Bible thousands of years ago to Dr. Kepple so we'd know we were on the right track. God is amazing, is He not?"

Sandy couldn't disagree with that statement. God was amazing. And so was Uncle Ralph sometimes.

"He's amazing, Uncle Ralph," he replied respectfully. "Truly amazing."

The sharp smell of the gasoline seared their nostrils, but they continued to carefully splash the contents of the large cans around Waldo's sweet shop until there wasn't any left. Then they returned the empty cans to the back of the truck.

"Now where was I? Ah, yes '... *wailing and gnashing of teeth. Then shall the righteous shine forth as the sun in the kingdom of their Father.*' Oh, then there's a bit about ears."

"Ears?"

"'*Who hath ears to hear, let him hear.*' That's about you, boy. You and your big ears."

"Me? God wrote about ME in the Bible?"

"Yep. That's why you get the honor of setting off the fireworks."

Uncle Ralph handed Sandy the matchbook, then climbed into the truck and turned it over.

"God wrote about each and every one of us in the Bible. When I was just a little shaver, my great-grand-pappy showed me the verse that refers to me."

Sandy struck a match, lit the whole matchbook, stared at it reverently – caught up for a moment in its heavenly brilliance – then tossed the thing into the dark, glistening pool of gasoline that had begun to leak out onto the back porch.

"It's in The Epistle to Philemon. It's a thing about refreshing my bowels in The Lord."

With an enthusiastic whoosh, the fuel ignited. Sandy, big ears red with excitement about a job well done, jumped into the truck cab and Uncle Ralph gunned the engine.

"At the time I never understood how the thing about refreshing my bowels in The Lord had anything to do with me personally – actually, I still don't quite understand it – but in time I have faith all be made clear."

With that, they were gone. They weren't going to hang around to watch it burn, of course. That would have been prideful and one shouldn't be prideful when serving The Lord.

Instead they went home to have a beer and watch it on the late news.

•

The village, of course, was too small for a proper professional fire department. Putting out the occasional blaze was done, as so much often is in small towns, by volunteers. Dedicated and extremely hard-working volunteers, of course. But volunteers nonetheless who must first be informed of the incident, then extricate themselves from whatever it is they are doing, make their way to the fire station, wrap up in their bulky protective gear, pack themselves into the fire engine and only then can they go to the fire. All too often, by the time they actually get to the fire, the conflagration has progressed too far for them to make much of a difference, except to, hopefully, prevent the flames from spreading.

And so it was this evening. Poor Waldo's sweet shop was a complete loss by the time they managed to arrive and it was only with considerable effort that they were able to save the surrounding structures.

By village standards, this sort of outcome was accounted a huge success and signal achievement. Understandably, certain selfishly self-interested parties didn't always share in this kind of opinion.

●

When Waldo was roused from his tear-drenched reverie by the sound of the fire engine he discovered that he had gravitated back to the park bench where he'd been accosted earlier that day by that flock of ravenous pigeons – but he could not rouse himself to take any interest as to why a fire engine might be roaming about this evening.

Instead, he fell back into his ponderous pondering. Perhaps he even slept a bit. In time, he came to realize that the sky had darkened. The moon had shifted and the few clouds no longer reflected flames.

Flames. There had been a fire, he now recognized. He remembered hearing a fire truck – and the concomitant commotion – but no longer. The village was at peace yet again.

He looked at his watch. His comfortable old watch that Mr. Hegge deprecated so. What a horrible man, that Mr. Hegge. Or perhaps not. Perhaps he only seemed horrible because Waldo was feeling so horrible himself at the time. Perhaps Mr. Hegge was a perfectly lovely fellow, with a wife and kids who adored him. It was possible.

Waldo knew it was time to go home. Time to crawl into bed. Even if he had to crawl into it all by himself.

And tomorrow? Tomorrow would be a new day, he struggled to assure himself, and he could start again. Perhaps his wife would come home and they could start again together. It was possible.

He got up eventually, dried his tears and shuffled off home, hoping not to run into anybody and never imagining what he might discover along the way.

•

The fire engine and its crew had left. The television news crew from the city had left. Mr. Hering and his annoying flashbulb had left. The village's few gapers and disaster fetishists had left.

And so, at this very moment, there was only Waldo, standing there all by himself in the fading moonlight.

When he finally registered what he was looking at, his knees grew weak and he collapsed in front of the still smoking ruins that were once his dear little sweet shop. For a long time he and a terrifyingly blank expression sat slumped up against the wall of Mr. Flick's butcher shop wondering why he could not weep. He should be weeping, shouldn't he? Or had he no more tears to spare? Was he fresh out?

Scattered about the street, soggy and torn owing to the firefighters' trampling about with firehoses, were horrifying hand-lettered and frightfully badly spelt placards accusing him of a wide variety of even worse crimes than he'd already been accused of. Apparently he was personally responsible for every evil known to or imagined by his fellow villagers. And now they'd gone and burned down his sweet shop.

Oh, why had he ever agreed to run for village council? He had hoped to do so much good, desperately wanted to do so much good. But now, now everything – everything – was quite utterly ruined. In the process, everything that had ever mattered to him had been torn from him. Ripped to shreds and now burnt. Burnt to cinders. He'd lost his wife, his friends, his good name, his livelihood and – and it was this sudden bizarre realization that finally opened the floodgates – even his beloved great-grandfather's antique silver scales with the arch little quote from *Much Ado About Nothing*. Their now melted, misshapen remains glittered reproachfully at him in the waning moonlight:

"*Hold you content,*" the elegant engraving had once so proudly proclaimed, "*...What, man! I know them, yea, | And what they weigh, even to the utmost scruple...*"

But no longer.

Now they were nothing but an ugly, useless lump of scrap metal. *Much Ado About Nothing,* indeed. Just like him.

With that awful insight, with those soul-crushing similes, the inescapable weight of the world at its most real bore down upon him and squeezed from him all that remained of his once enormous capacity to Hope.

As the wee hours grew larger and just before they exploded into the dawn of a brilliant new day, he came to the eventually tearless understanding that there was nothing left for him here but to bow crisply and make his exit, as Mr. Carle had seemed to suggest.

And so he did.

There in a bitter, blackened wilderness far, far away from the sweet little village in which he once thought he lived, helped by a shard of shattered glass pried from the remains of his shop's bay window, Emerson Waldo's great heart finally bled dry.

•

As was to be expected, those few who continued to believe in Waldo grieved much and those who knew him to be a monster rejoiced with an insufferable smugness.

His funeral was intended to be a quiet affair – no one really likes to be reminded of a death like that even if you couldn't bring yourself to approve of the person – but then Councilor Millstone announced that he would personally deliver the eulogy.

This came as a huge relief to Pastor Pat who was dreading the responsibility of verbally balancing so many competing goods and evils. Mrs. Waldo had been a loyal member of his congregation for years and he felt a certain professional responsibility to assuage her grief – but so many of his flock now hated Mr. Waldo with a (to his lights) decidedly un-Christ-like passion. Pastor Pat had been beside himself with worry and stress as he weighed the pros and cons of his being the sole provider of the eulogy. But his prayers had been answered by Councilor Millstone. It was no longer his responsibility, praise the Lord.

The councilor's unexpected willingness to involve himself in Waldo's memorial was immediately and widely regarded as tribute to the fine, unselfish nature of the good councilor and everyone in the village determined to attend and hear the Important Address that the councilor would no doubt deliver. Not one voter was disappointed. Although no one could quite remember what it was he said, nor whether it was pro- or anti-Waldo, it was roundly agreed that the councilor had a way with words and that it was always a pleasure to listen to him. Very restful was the happy consensus and it came as no surprise when he was re-elected in a landslide when the time for the actual voting came.

Mrs. Waldo blamed herself, of course, for her husband's demise and took to drink. Dr. and Mrs. Kepple decided to take a break from the political life and concentrate solely on charity work. Mr. Stieffel, who found himself profiting in the end, decided that saying nothing was best. And Mr. Carle decided to name the runt in the newest litter "Waldo" and to feed him by hand.

Oh, and despite the bit about the righteous shining forth, Uncle Ralph and Sandy had been carefully taught to be modest about their few accomplishments and never took a lick of credit for their small part in purging the world of iniquity.

It was, they understood, the Christian thing to do.

•

A few weeks after the funeral, Mr. Hering received a phone call from a nationally known Professor who made her home in the village, but taught at the university in the city. She wanted to discuss the ramifications of Waldo's foray into politics. Mr. Hering was putting together yet another piece on Waldo's gruesome suicide and thought this might add an interesting twist or two. The Professor went on for some time explaining her qualifications to pontificate, but Mr. Hering was finally forced to insist on getting down to brass tacks.

"Yes, yes, so what do you think of the whole Waldo Affair?" demanded Mr. Hering impatiently.

"The poor man was an Innocent," replied the Professor, who was a little put off by the newspaperman's obvious disinterest in her credentials. "Clearly he had no business in politics. But then we as a society create these tragedies. It's an ancient archetypal symbol drama we work through time and time again."

Mr. Hering couldn't remember if "archetypal" had an "e" in the middle of it or not. "Oh, well," he thought, "my spell checker will sort that out."

"It's rather like tossing a virgin into a volcano or tacking up on a cross a lecturer you don't particularly care for. In academic circles it happens all the time, we don't even bat an eyelid about it anymore. No, I'm sorry to say it, but Waldo's wants and desires, his potential contributions as a village councilor were ultimately irrelevant. Waldo himself was unimportant, except as he could serve as one of those periodic sacrifices that the public hungers for, that the public seems to desperately need. It's an ancient thing, and tragic in a sense that predates the Greek. It's almost primeval. Indeed, probably is. Fascinating phenomenon we almost invariably transform into a sacred transaction. A Goat of Azazel thing, you know – Day of Atonement and all? I'm writing a paper on it, actually. Waldo's death, unfortunate as it was, was an excellent illustration of this point in a contemporary context. Frankly, it couldn't come at a more opportune time in my researches."

"You sound pretty callous, Professor." Mr. Hering bristled.

"Yes, I suppose it sounds that way to a layman," noted the Professor soothingly. "Academics and medical doctors are so used to dealing with the dread-full side of humanity, we are forced to develop rather more scar tissue than the average fellow. It's the same with the police. Surely you yourself as a newspaperman have had some experience with the phenomenon?"

"Well, yes, I –."

"As I was saying, Mr. Hering, we always seem to forget that ancient archetypal symbols live in everyday, ordinary experience. The awe, for example, in which we hold Mother Teresa is not unlike the awe felt by ancient Babylonians for what we inaccurately term their temple prostitutes, who were in fact highly honored and much sanctified priestesses of their particular deity. No, Mr. Hering, the human experience of the sacred is indivisible, when viewed with enough perspective."

Mr. Hering was on the whole disappointed with the professor's ramblings and decided not to use them in his piece on Waldo's passing. To be frank, Mr. Hering hated intellectuals, especially those who talked in circles without ever making themselves clear to ordinary people. However, he didn't want to waste the interview entirely, so he pasted together a few of the more interesting quotes from the public's perspective and slipped them into a highly successful article on the entertainment page a few weeks later under the headline, "Feminist Professor Links Mother Teresa to Ritualized Prostitution."

•

A few months later Chief Gunderson was forced into early retirement thanks to a vigorous campaign chaired by Regina Dolack. She had never forgiven him for having put a pantless suspected child molester in a cell with her pantless eleven-year-old boy. And then released the damned child molester.

(Little Ricky had learned a very important lesson that day. His mother had been right – they usually are about such things – one should always wear clean underwear. You can never predict what's coming down nor when nor with whom.)

That it *wasn't* the Chief who had locked Ricky up in the first place wasn't deemed pertinent. That it *was* the Chief had let him go also wasn't deemed pertinent. That Waldo hadn't been convicted of any impropriety wasn't deemed pertinent either. Nor was Principal MacNulty's Zero Tolerance policy with regard to plastic butter knives brought into any serious question. People were outraged, thanks to the justifiably outraged Mrs. Dolack's efforts and a head had to roll. It was the Chief's because he was officially "in charge". Besides Deputy Noakes was only on loan to the village and contractually couldn't possibly be held responsible or punished. (The village's attorney, Mr. King had patiently explained all that to the campaign committee.) More to the point, a considerable number of folks (which is to say voters) still regarded the deputy as a hero for having saved the little girl from Waldo even though it wasn't Waldo from whom she'd needed saved.

And so it was Chief Gunderson who was put out to pasture. (Literally. He'd inherited his Uncle Gustav's farm some years previously and that's where he went.) After all the viciousness directed in his direction with regard to the unfortunate incident, he decided he was on the whole relieved to leave public service. The world of law enforcement was no longer what it was when he had been rookie cop. An unprepared but enthusiastic Elmo took his place until a replacement could be found. One could not found and so it was Elmo who became Chief in the course of time. Deputy Noakes (thanks to all the publicity) was offered and took a job with an at once exceedingly secret yet highly publicized government agency and enjoyed a distinguished career there rooting out and neutralizing *suspected* terrorists until it was discovered that he occasionally fudged his expense reports.

Principal MacNulty, we should also note, went on to considerable national notoriety, writing a best-selling book and traveling the talk show circuit, as a result of removing all the dictionaries from school classrooms because the word "sex" had been defined in them. The Principal insisted that defining "sex" was tantamount to sex education which had been clearly forbidden by order of the school board. It was a controversial interpretation on his part, but happily the controversy only sold more of his books.

•

Six months after Waldo's death, when Councilor Millstone left for an undisclosed tropical isle with the entire village treasury and his neighbor's sixteen-year-old daughter, it came as a great shock to the village. But soon enough people began saying things like, "It was to be expected. After all he was a politician!" and "I never liked him anyway!" and "I told you so, didn't I?" and, not surprisingly, "Thank goodness we didn't elect Waldo – at least with Millstone, the girl was sixteen!"

And in another six months Mr. Hering solemnly announced in *The Herald Sentinel Gazette* an earth-shaking discovery made by means of a scientific poll the newspaper had commissioned "at considerable expense" from a prestigious research firm in the city. The poll indicated that absolutely no one had voted for Councilor Millstone. However, after the rather startled researchers put the data through a rigorous and extensive analysis process – as well as asked a few more questions – it emerged that although people clearly had voted for the councilor, no one had been willing to admit it.

"Surely we must all have voted for him," mused Mr. Hering in his best slice-of-life-slash-human-interest editorial style. "For he was elected in a Landslide. It all comes down to Human Nature, doesn't it? No one likes to admit they made a mistake. But in this instance whose fault was it? What real choice had we at the ballot box? Until better people choose to run, the body politic will continue to be victimized by the Unscrupulous and the Criminal. It's very sad, indeed tragic, but nothing can be gained by rehashing what happened – nothing can be changed by beating ourselves up. We're not the guilty party here! We're just doing the best that we can. Our goal today must be to move on, to forgive and forget. To find closure. We have a nice little village here full of good, decent people and we should be proud of it and each other no matter what our occasional little failings are."

Down at the barbershop and village tavern each man shook his head as he looked over the edge of his paper at his neighbor and contemplated and enumerated that neighbor's innumerable deficiencies in the warm glow of a newfound and surprisingly congenial charity. At the Beauty Shoppe, the ladies dabbed their eyes as Betty Sue read out the editorial and even Mrs. Windsor and Mrs. King (*née* Hagelboot) kissed and forgave each other their various (they now realized) overheated remarks. And soon enough, Life settled back down to normal and everyone lived happily ever after, except for Waldo.

Except for Waldo, of course...

about the author

Over the course of the last half century NURMI HUSA *has been a professional actor on the stage, over the airwaves and in film – as well as a designer, visual artist, writer, editor, director, photographer, political activist, file clerk, property manager, computer programmer and, perhaps most horrifying of all, the assistant manager of a dilapidated movie theatre in Hollywood.*

Oh, and a godfather. Best job of them all.